KRIEGSMARINE

The illustrated history of the German Navy in WWII

KRIEGSMARINE

The illustrated history of the German Navy in WWII

Robert Jackson

MBI Publishing Company

This edition first published in 2001
by MBI Publishing Company
729 Prospect Avenue, PO Box 1, Osceola, WI 54020-0001 USA

The information in this book is true and complete to the best of our knowledge. All recommendations are made without any guarantee on the part of the author or publisher, who also disclaim any liability incurred in connection with the use of this data or specific details.

We recognize that some words, model names and designations, for example, mentioned herein are the property of the trademark holder. We use them for identification purposes only. This is not an official publication.

MBI Publishing Company books are also available at discounts in bulk quantity for industrial or sales-promotional use. For details write the Special Sales Manager at Motorbooks International Wholesalers & Distributors, 729 Prospect Avenue, PO Box 1, Osceola, WI 54020-0001 USA.

Library of Congress Cataloging-in-Publication Data available.

ISBN 0 7603 1026 2

Editorial and design by
Amber Books Ltd
Bradley's Close
74–77 White Lion Street
London N1 9PF

Project Editor: Naomi Waters
Designer: Brian Rust
Picture Research: Lisa Wren

Printed in Italy - Nuova GEP, Cremona

Page 1: *On 18 April 1939 units of the German fleet set out for a one-month training voyage. The armoured cruisers* Admiral Graf Spee *and* Deutschland *are seen here passing through the English Channel between Folkestone and Calais.*
Page 2: *A German U-boat returns from an operational voyage and makes for its base on the French Atlantic coast.*

CONTENTS

CHAPTER 1

REBIRTH 6

CHAPTER 2

U-BOATS 28

CHAPTER 3

COMMERCE RAIDERS 58

CHAPTER 4

FAST ATTACK – THE S-BOATS 78

CHAPTER 5

CAPITAL SHIPS 96

CHAPTER 6

CRUISERS AND DESTROYERS 122

CHAPTER 7

ESCORT VESSELS 152

INDEX 174

CHAPTER 1
REBIRTH

In 1919, the once-proud Imperial German fleet lay in ruins, its warships at the bottom of the sea, scuttled by their crews. Yet, only two decades later, the German Navy had again become a major challenge on the high seas.

Left: The launching of the German 'pocket battleship' Admiral Graf Spee *at Wilhelmshaven, on 30 June 1934. Properly named 'armoured ships',* Graf Spee *and her two sisters,* Deutschland *and* Admiral Scheer, *were designed as fast commerce raiders.*

Above: After the Battle of Jutland on 31 May 1916, the German High Seas Fleet spent the remainder of World War I mostly penned up in its home ports. The harbour shown here is unidentified, but is probably Wilhelmshaven.

On 21 November 1918, 10 days after the signing of the Armistice that brought to an end the bloodiest war in human history, the main body of the German High Seas Fleet (HSF) sailed under escort from its North German bases to surrender to the Allies at Scapa Flow, the Royal Navy's anchorage in the Orkney Islands. For more than two years, since the Battle of Jutland in May 1916, the principal units of the German Fleet had lain mostly idle, their personnel racked by revolt in the latter weeks of the war. Now, still undefeated in battle, nine battleships, five battlecruisers, seven light cruisers and 49 destroyers sailed past the massive armada of British, French and American warships that had been assembled off Rosyth, in the mouth of the Firth of Forth, sailed on for the Orkney Island base, and dropped anchor at their designated places. Then came the final humiliation, in the form of a signal from Admiral Beatty, Commander-in-Chief of the British Grand Fleet.

'The German flag is to be hauled down at 1557 today, Thursday, and is not to be hoisted again without permission.'

Vice-Admiral Ludwig von Reuter, the German commander, protested in vain about this instruction. Beatty's blunt response was that a state of war still existed between Britain and Germany, and that no enemy vessel therefore could fly its flag in a British port.

The end of the Imperial German Navy

In April 1919, while the German warships and their crews continued to languish in Scapa Flow, cut off from the outside world and receiving only basic rations and scanty communications from

Left: *A battle squadron of the Imperial German Navy in line astern in the North Sea. This photo was most probably taken from a Zeppelin of the German Naval Airship Division, whose main task was to cooperate with surface units.*

Right: *Vice-Admiral Adolf von Trotha became the High Seas Fleet Chief of Staff in 1916, and was head of the German Admiralty in 1919. The following year, he was responsible for organizing the* Reichsmarine, *which formed the basis for future expansion.*

Below: *Warships of the Royal Navy, with main armament trained, escort units of the HSF to their internment at Scapa Flow. Allied vacillation over the fate of the German fleet led to the ships being scuttled by their crews.*

Above: The Kaiser-*class dreadnought* Kaiserin *being broken up at Rosyth in 1936 after salvage. The vessel is still inverted. Note the massive turret for her twin 30.5cm (12in) guns.* Kaiserin *was one of the first German battleships to be fitted with turbines.*

Top right: The propeller of the German battleship Bayern *photographed after the vessel had been towed to the breaker's yard at Rosyth in the Firth of Forth. The hulk was refloated in September 1934.*

Germany, an 'interim' German Navy was established under the command of Vice-Admiral von Trotha. Two months later, on 21 June 1919 – the deadline by which the future of the German High Seas Fleet was to have been decided by the Allied and German delegations at Versailles, where a peace treaty was being negotiated – the German warships were scuttled by their crews at Scapa Flow on the orders of Admiral von Reuter. Only the battleship *Baden* and a few destroyers were saved by British boarding parties. It was the end of the Imperial German Navy.

In fact, the beginning of the end had come in the wake of the Battle of Jutland, a massive engagement involving 259 warships; the Royal Navy had suffered a numerical defeat, losing more warships and men than the Germans, but had gained a strategic

Left: *Lashed to tugs, the* Bayern, *still inverted, in passage from Scapa Flow to Rosyth. Refloating the scuttled High Seas Fleet was a massive undertaking. Only one battleship and a few destroyers escaped being scuttled by their crews.*

Above: *Raising the German battlecruiser* Hindenburg *at Scapa Flow in July 1930 for scrap. She was still of sufficient interest to be examined in some detail by the Royal Corps of Naval Constructors.*

Above: '*Running on the spot – commence!*' *German sailors at their physical training on the deck of a German battleship in 1916. At this stage of the war, the morale of the High Seas Fleet was high; at the end of the war, sailors felt betrayed by their superiors, because they had never been decisively defeated in battle.*

Top left: *At Jutland, a British shell tore this massive hole through the armour of the* Derfflinger, *below the bridge. The battlecruiser took 21 hits and suffered extensive damage, but remained afloat.*

Below left: *Sailors of the High Seas Fleet demonstrating in Kiel following receipt of the Allied demand to surrender the German warships. By the end of World War I, the Imperial German Navy was in a state of mutiny.*

victory in that the High Seas Fleet retreated to its main base at Wilhelmshaven, and never ventured out in strength again. Only in October 1918, as the war drew to its inevitable conclusion, did the German admirals plan to emerge for a fight to the finish in the North Sea, a suicidal scheme that provoked open mutiny on the German warships at Kiel and Wilhelmshaven.

As far as the German Navy was concerned, the restrictions imposed by the Versailles Peace Treaty – which ironically was formalized only a week after the fleet scuttled itself at Scapa Flow – were little short of draconian. It would not be permitted to have a submarine service, which was an understandable condition given the terrible losses inflicted on Allied merchant shipping in World War I by German submarines; neither would it be allowed to develop a postwar naval air arm. In fact, when the Allies demand-

Above: The old battleships Hessen *(left) and* Schleswig-Holstein *at Palermo, Sicily, during a courtesy visit. The* Schleswig-Holstein *would later fire the opening shots of World War II.*

ed the surrender of further capital ships to compensate for those scuttled at Scapa Flow, the German Navy was reduced to a coastal defence force, armed with a motley collection of obsolete warships which included eight old pre-war battleships, eight light cruisers, 32 destroyers and torpedo boats, some minesweepers, and auxiliary craft. If new capital ships were built in the future to replace the old vessels, their displacement was not to exceed 10,000 tons, while that of new-build cruisers was to be no greater than 6,000 tons.

Modest beginnings

In organizing his new navy, Admiral von Trotha was faced with a set of serious problems. For one thing, thousands of personnel of the former Imperial German Navy, banded together under the banner of the *Marinefreikorps* (Naval Free Corps), were fighting what amounted to a civil war against insurgent communists and radical socialists. The *Marinefreikorps* later changed its identity to the Brigade Erhardt and, becoming involved in a pro-monarchist revolt against the governing Weimar Republic – the so-called Second Reich, established after the abdication of Kaiser Wilhelm II –

occupied Berlin on 13 March 1920. The socialists prevailed, and the Weimar leaders, seeing von Trotha as a potential threat, forced the admiral to resign as head of the *Reichsmarine*.

In October 1920, he was replaced by Admiral Paul Behnke, whose priority task was to restructure the *Reichsmarine*, and to train a future generation of naval officers. To this end, a *Bildungsinspektion* – Training Department – was created within the *Reichsmarine*, directed by an officer who had entered the Imperial Navy in 1894 and seen action at the Battle of the Dogger Bank in World War I. He was Rear-Admiral Erich Raeder.

The principal aim of the *Reichsmarine*, as defined in a memo of September 1920, was to assure the integrity of Germany's coastline, although there was a provision for its warships to carry out courtesy visits overseas to 'show the flag' and to enhance crew training. At the same time, the government made funds available for the start of a modest shipbuilding programme, and also for refitting some of the old Imperial Navy warships. The battleships *Braunschweig*, *Elsass*, *Hannover*, and *Hessen* were all refitted and rearmed in the early 1920s, while two others, *Schlesien* and *Schleswig-Holstein*, were reconstructed at a later date. The first German warship to be built from scratch after World War I, the light cruiser *Emden*, was laid down in 1921, but due to the country's confused political and economic climate, she took four years to complete. She was launched on 7 January 1925 at the Wilhelmshaven Dockyard. Originally coal-fired, she converted to oil

Right: Vice-Admiral Hans Zenker, head of the Reichsmarine, *pictured in 1928. At this time, France, as Poland's ally, was deemed to be Germany's most likely future enemy, so the* Reichsmarine's *primary concerns were to maintain the free flow of German North Sea shipping, and prevent a French force entering the Baltic. It was under Zenker's authority that Germany first began to build the new light cruisers, destroyers and torpedo boats to perform these tasks.*

Below: German sailors disembarking at Wilhelmshaven in 1920 after their release from internment in Britain following the scuttling of the High Seas Fleet at Scapa Flow. Many of these seamen would go on to play key roles in the next war.

Above: The light cruiser Emden *was the first medium-sized warship built in Germany after World War I. She was not of great fighting value, and served as a training ship before World War II.*

in 1934. Designed primarily for foreign service, with crew training in mind, she made nine foreign cruises as a training ship from 1926.

The first new-build ships

In 1924, Admiral Behnke was replaced as head of the *Reichsmarine* by Vice-Admiral Hans Zenker, and under his authority, to replace the worn out World War I torpedo boats then in service, the construction of 12 new torpedo boats was started, six of the *Raubvogel* (Bird of Prey) class and six of the *Raubtier* (Predator) class, all at the Wilhelmshaven Dockyard. The *Raubvogel* class comprised the *Albatros*, *Falke* (Falcon), *Greif* (Griffin), *Kondor*, *Seeadler* (Sea Eagle) and *Möwe* (Seagull), while the six ships of the *Raubtier* class

Right: Admiral Erich Raeder was Chief of Naval Staff from 1928 to 1935, and Commander-in-Chief of the Kriegsmarine *until 1943. Although he opposed a two-front war, he remained loyal to Hitler and recommended the beginning of unrestricted submarine warfare. Tried at Nuremberg, Raeder was sentenced to life imprisonment, but was released in 1955. He died in 1960.*

Above: Reichsmarine *officers undergoing theoretical training at the Naval Officers' School in Mürwick. German instruction was very thorough and embraced all the most modern knowledge. The stringent training syllabus was not relaxed until critical manpower shortages made it necessary.*

were the *Iltis* (Polecat), *Jaguar*, *Leopard*, *Luchs* (Lynx), *Tiger*, and *Wolf*. With a displacement of around 930 tons, these vessels, classed as destroyers under the terms of the Versailles Treaty, were powered by two-shaft geared turbines and were capable of 41km/h (22 knots). All were armed with six 53cm (21in) torpedo tubes, three 10.4cm (4.1in) guns and four 20mm AA guns. They carried a complement of 129, and all were completed by 1929. The priority given to the construction of light cruisers and torpedo boats during this period arose from a conviction that, in the event of any future confrontation between Germany and Poland, the latter's ally, France, might pose the main naval threat; the assumption was

that Britain and the United States would remain neutral. Fast, light cruisers and torpedo boats were regarded as the warships most suited to the task of keeping French warships out of the Baltic, and of escorting German mercantile shipping in the North Sea.

The rise of Erich Raeder

In the late 1920s, the *Reichsmarine* found itself in the middle of a political storm when the German Socialist Party (SPD) discovered that plans were being laid to build a new class of warship. In the 1928 *Reichstag* elections, the SPD campaigned under the slogan 'Food not *Panzerkreuzer*'. Known initially as *Panzerkreuzer* (armoured cruisers) and later as *Panzerschiffe* (armoured ships), they were designed from the start as commerce raiders, with a large and economical radius of action of 16,677km/9,000nm at 35km/h (19 knots). In order to comply with the maximum tonnage specified by the various naval treaties of the 1920s, they were electrically welded to save weight and equipped with diesel

engines. They had enough speed – 48km/h (26 knots) – to enable them to escape from any vessel that could not be overwhelmed by their guns. Their armament comprised six 28cm (11in), eight 15cm (5.9in), six 10.4cm (4.1in) AA, eight 37mm AA, 10 (later 28) 20mm AA guns and eight 53cm (21in) torpedo tubes. They carried a complement of 1,150.

Such was the weight of public opinion against the cost involved in building these warships that Admiral Zenker was replaced by Admiral Erich Raeder, an officer who was considered to be more acceptable to all political parties, and who had left the Training Department in 1924 to become head of the Baltic Station, one of the three top positions in the *Reichsmarine*. Raeder had served as a staff officer to Admiral Franz von Hipper towards the end of World War I, and had later been assigned the task of writing two volumes of the official German history of the war at sea, a work he completed whilst lying low in the Naval Historical Library,

following an accusation that he had been involved in the Navy-backed Berlin uprising of 1920. These volumes dealt with the activities of the German commerce raiders in distant waters during the war, and it was only while compiling this account that Raeder had become fully aware of the damage these vessels had inflicted on Allied shipping. Not only that; they had also tied down large numbers of Allied capital ships and cruisers, diverted to search for them.

The first of the new armoured ships, known initially as *Schiff A* or *Ersatz Preussen*, was laid down by Deutsche Werke, Kiel on 5 February 1929. (The *Preussen*, the battleship she was to replace, as indicated by her designation, was stricken in April 1929 and scrapped in 1931.) The new warship displaced 11,700 tons and was officially named *Deutschland* at her launch on 19 May 1931. A second vessel in the class was laid down at Wilhelmshaven as the *Ersatz Lothringen* on 25 June 1931, and was launched on 1 April 1933, receiving the name *Admiral Scheer*, and a third, also laid down at Wilhelmshaven on 1 October 1932 as the *Ersatz Braunschweig*, was named *Admiral Graf Spee* at her launch on 30 June

1934. There is little doubt that more of these fast, efficient 'pocket battleships' would have been ordered had not a change of naval policy followed the rise to power of Hitler and the National Socialist German Labour Party (NSDAP) in 1933.

Naval expansion under Hitler

The 1932 Geneva disarmament conference, to which a German delegation was invited for the first time, paid little attention to naval matters, focussing instead on the size and composition of land forces. Meanwhile, the German government had approved what was referred to as a *Schiffsbauersatzplan* (replacement ship-building programme), which envisaged the building up of a new German naval force in two phases, the first spanning the years 1930–36, and the second 1936–1943. The second phase was

Below: One of the first volunteers for the new German **Kriegsmarine** *is signed on. There was no shortage of young men waiting to come forward. This one appears to have had previous military training; he is standing correctly to attention.*

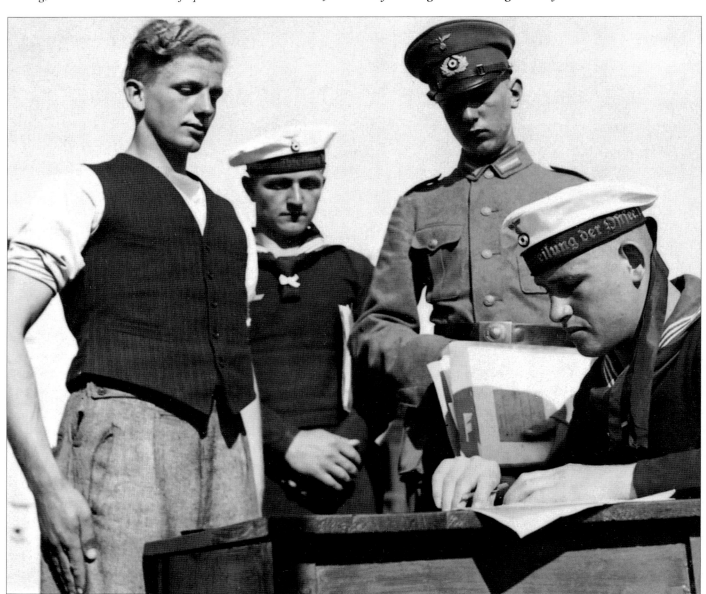

Above: Taken in December 1935, this photograph shows a batch of Kriegsmarine *volunteers being allocated their bunks on arrival at Wilhelmshaven. Hitler reintroduced conscription in this year, partly as a means of solving the unemployment problem.*

secret, and it was under its umbrella that Adolf Hitler would launch a major warship construction plan as part of his scheme to repudiate the Versailles Treaty and establish Germany as a world naval power.

The German shipbuilding programme proceeded slowly, partly because the new Chancellor realized that to accelerate it would almost certainly provoke a furious reaction from Britain and the other former belligerents, but mainly because of economic constraints. All the maritime nations were feeling the effects of a severe economic depression, and were eager to escape the cost of building replacement capital ships; economies imposed by the naval treaties of the early 1930s were dictated by necessity, rather than a genuine desire for disarmament. In any event, by the end of 1933, it was apparent that disarmament was a fast-receding goal. In that year, Japan invaded Manchuria, precipitating a landslide of aggressive actions by other nations which would lead to the dismemberment of the League of Nations, which had been formed in 1919 in the

hope of bringing peace and stability to a broken world.

At the core of Germany's early naval expansion programme were the light cruisers. The *Emden* of 1925 has already been mentioned; she was followed in 1927 by the *Karlsrühe*, launched in 1927, the *Köln* of 1928 and the *Leipzig* of 1929. Next came the *Nürnberg*, launched in 1934, and the *Königsberg* in 1937. The *Nürnberg* and *Leipzig*, at 6,700 tons, were the largest, with a complement of 850 men. Their armament comprised nine 15cm (5.9in), eight 8.9cm (3.5in) AA, and eight 37mm AA, as well as 12 53cm (21in) torpedo tubes, and they had a top speed of 59km/h (32 knots). The others were smaller, displacing 5,600 tons and with a complement of 630 men. They carried an armament of eight 15cm (5.9in), three 8.9cm (3.5in) AA and four 37mm AA guns, in addition to four 53cm (21in) torpedo tubes. Three other light cruisers, which remained unnamed, were never finished and were broken up on their stocks in 1943, and three more remained projects only.

With the Nazi Party in power in Germany there came a change of naval strategy. France was regarded as the potential enemy of the future, and a strategy for the conduct of naval warfare in the Atlantic was the main consideration. The immediate result was the construction of a new class of *Schlachtkreuzer* (Battlecruiser). Five

Above: The light cruiser Leipzig *on exercise in the North Sea in 1934. The* Leipzig *survived World War II, despite being badly damaged on two occasions, and was sunk in the Baltic in 1946, laden with canisters of poison gas.*

Below: The old pre-dreadnought battleships, Schlesien *and* Schleswig-Holstein, *at Kiel. They were the only capital ships Germany was allowed to retain under the terms of the Versailles Treaty, which went on to be active during World War II.*

ships were projected, but only two were started. The first of these, the 32,000-ton *Scharnhorst*, was laid down at Wilhelmshaven in April 1934; she was followed a year later by the *Gneisenau*.

The design of these powerful warships was based on that of the uncompleted *Mackensen*-class battlecruisers of World War I, which in turn were based on the *Derfflinger* of 1912 – arguably the best battlecruiser of its day. The new ships were fitted with three-shaft geared turbines and their radius of action was 18,530 km (10,000nm) at 35km/h (19 knots). Their armament comprised nine 28cm (11in), 12 15cm (5.9in), 14 10.5cm (4.1in), 37mm AA, and 10 (later 38) 20mm AA guns, as well as six 53cm (21in) torpedo tubes. Each carried four spotter aircraft and had a complement of 1,800. They were capable of a speed of 57km/h (31 knots). *Scharnhorst* was launched in October 1936 and *Gneisenau* in December the same year. By this time, in May 1935, the *Reichsmarine* (Reich Navy) had been renamed the *Kriegsmarine* (War Navy), reflecting Hitler's determination to break free of the last shackles of the Treaty of Versailles.

In the mid-1930s, a new class of *Schwerer Kreuzer* (heavy cruiser) was also laid down. There were five ships in all, named *Lützow*, *Seydlitz*, *Prinz Eugen*, *Blücher*, and *Admiral Hipper*. The first-

Below: The battlecruiser Scharnhorst *under construction at Bremen in 1934. Based on the uncompleted* Mackensen-*class battlecruisers, the* Scharnhorst *and her sister* Gneisenau *were among the most powerful warships in the world.*

named, launched in July 1939, was sold in 1940 to the Soviet Navy, in whose service she was successively named *Petropavlovsk* and *Tallinn*. The others were all launched between 1937 and 1939. Capable of 59km/h (32 knots), their armament comprised eight 20cm (8in), 12 10.5cm (4.1in) AA, 12 37mm AA, and eight (later 28) 20mm AA guns, in addition to 12 53cm (21in) torpedo tubes. Each carried three spotter aircraft. Complement was 1,600.

Hitler's new battleships

In the late 1930s, German naval strategy still revolved around the possibility of a future conflict in the Atlantic, and the Munich Crisis of 1938 led Hitler – who had a very detailed knowledge of naval tehcnology – to believe that there was now the prospect of a naval confrontation with Britain. To be assured of naval supremacy on the high seas he needed a fleet of super-powerful battleships, two of which had already been laid down in 1936. These were the *Bismarck* and *Tirpitz*, respectively laid down as *Schiff F Ersatz Hannover* and *Schiff G Ersatz Schleswig-Holstein*. Displacing 41,700 tons in the case of *Bismarck* and 42,900 tons in the case of *Tirpitz*, they would have a speed of 54km/h (29 knots), and a combat radius of 16,677km (9,000nm) at 35km/h (19 knots). They would carry a formidable armament of eight 38cm (15in), 12 15cm (5.9in), 16 10.5cm (4.1in) AA, 16 37mm AA and 16 (later 58) 20mm AA guns, together with eight 53cm (21in) torpedo tubes. Their complement would be 2,400 officers and men. Six even larger (56,200-ton) battleships were planned, known simply by

the letters H, J, K, L, M and N. Only H and J were laid down, in 1938, and these were broken up on the stocks in the summer of 1940, at a time when Germany believed she had won the war.

The lack of naval air power

One obvious deficiency in Germany's naval inventory at the time of Hitler's rise to power in 1933 was that it did not include an aircraft carrier. Plans for one were drawn up without any input from the *Luftwaffe*, which showed no enthusiasm for the project, and in December 1936 construction began of the 23,200-ton *Graf Zeppelin*. She was launched in December 1938, but never finished; after many delays, work was halted in 1940 when she was 85 per cent complete. Her four-shaft geared turbines would have given her a maximum speed of 61km/h (33 knots), and a combat radius of 14,824km (8,000nm) at 35km/h (19 knots). In its finalized form, her air group was to have comprised 28 Junkers Ju87D and 12 Messerschmitt Me109Gs fighters. The hull of a sister vessel was completed up to the armoured deck but was never launched, and

Above: The German caption on the back of this photograph, which shows a reconnaissance floatplane on its catapult aboard the battlecruiser Gneisenau, *states that the aircraft is an Arado Ar-196. It is, in fact, a Heinkel He 114, which was eventually replaced by the Ar-196.*

broken up on the stocks in 1940. It was speculated that this ship was to have been named *Peter Strasser*, after the commander of the German Naval Airship Division in World War I.

A new generation of destroyers

The lack of a modern destroyer force also gave concern to Germany's naval planners in the mid-1930s, and two new classes were laid down; the *Leberecht Maass* class (16 ships) and the *Diether von Roeder* (6 ships), all named after sailors who had been honoured in World War I. Designed for operations in the North Sea and the Baltic, they were destined to see World War II service in all waters from Biscay to the Arctic.

Above: *The armoured ship ('pocket battleship') Admiral Graf Spee, suitably bedecked at the naval review held at Spithead on 20 May 1937 to celebrate the coronation of His Majesty King George VI. The ship is carrying a Heinkel He 60 floatplane.*

Below: *A Signalmeister (Signalman) communicating with the battlecruiser Gneisenau. Although the Scharnhorst and Gneisenau were classed as battlecruisers by the Allies, the Germans always referred to them as battleships.*

The secret development of submarines

In one area, and in conditions of strict secrecy, German naval experts had been operating in defiance of the Versailles Treaty for years before Hitler came to power. In 1922, operating from clandestine offices in the Netherlands and Spain, German submarine designers and constructors, under the guise of offering submersibles for service with foreign navies, began work on undersea craft which, in the fullness of time, would serve as prototypes for a new generation of German U-boats. One such craft, built for the Turkish Navy, became the prototype for two 862-ton Type IA U-boats built in 1936, while a submarine constructed for Finland was actually the prototype for the Type IIA U-boat. Another Finnish boat served as the prototype for what was to become the main operational U-boat class, the Type VII.

Above: The launch of the aircraft carrier Graf Zeppelin *at Kiel on 8 December 1938. Never completed, the* Graf Zeppelin *vanished in unknown circumstances (probably hit by a mine) while being towed to Leningrad by the Soviets after World War II.*

It was in these small, 25-man foreign boats that Hitler's newly appointed U-boat commander, Captain Karl Dönitz, set about training his submarine crews. After 16 March 1935, Hitler formally repudiated the Treaty of Versailles; a U-boat construction programme was started in Germany, helped on its way by a rather curious naval agreement between England and Germany that permitted the Germans to build submarine tonnage up to 45 per cent of the Royal Navy's. This agreement, concluded in June 1935 without consultation with the Dominions, France or the United States, opened the door for a massive increase in Germany's submarine fleet; yet by August 1939, the *Kriegsmarine* still had only 56 submarines, of which 22 were ocean-going craft.

There seemed to be time enough for the naval build-up to proceed to the point where Germany's surface and submarine fleet would be more than capable of destroying the commerce of Britain and her allies, if hostilities broke out. The German naval planners, after all, had never envisaged having to fight a major war before 1944. They had reckoned without Hitler's ambitions in the east, and the determined stance of Britain and her allies.

War would be thrust upon them within weeks, rather than years.

Right: Leberecht Maass-class (1934 Type) destroyers at their moorings. Sixteen of this 2000-ton class were built, and 10 were sunk in World War II. Not originally designed for oceanic warfare, they operated in all conditions around Nazi-occupied Europe.

Below: Type II U-boats at the Naval Training School in Kiel. All the boats seen here, which were used exclusively for training purposes, survived World War II, and were subsequently paid off or scrapped.

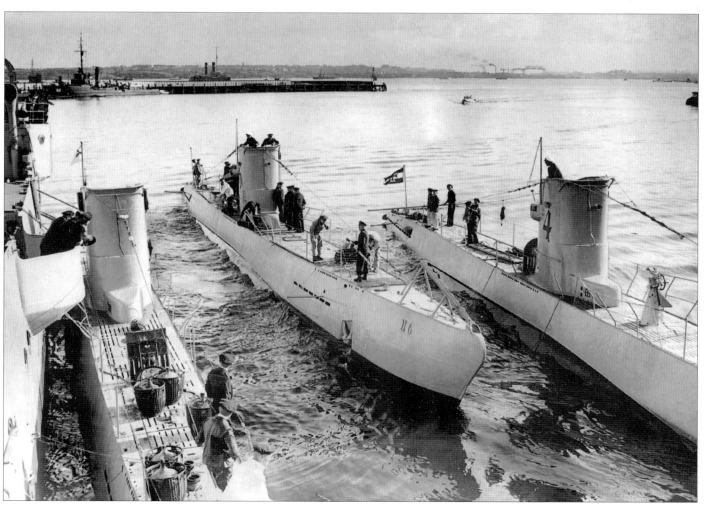

U-BOATS

From the very beginning of World War II, the German U-boats presented the most serious threat to Allied shipping. The Allies won the Battle of the Atlantic, but the cost in ships, aircraft and lives was enormous.

On 19 August 1939, in anticipation that Britain and France would declare war on Germany following the latter's imminent invasion of Poland, the German Naval High Command (*Oberkommando der Kriegsmarine*, or OKM) dispatched 14 ocean-going Type VII and IX U-boats to the North Atlantic, ready to begin operations against Allied merchant ships. Eleven more U-boats stood ready to carry out minelaying operations off the British Isles, while a similar number lay in wait to the west of the Bay of Biscay, covering the approaches to the French Atlantic ports. Ten more, mostly Type IIs, were on station in the Baltic.

Left: Pictured in 1938, a German U-boat travels at speed on the surface during an exercise in the Baltic. Germany still possessed only a relatively small number of submarines at the outbreak of World War II; 14 of them were deployed for attacks on Allied commerce and 11 more for minelaying operations.

Above: Kapitanleutnant Brautigam, commander of the German submarine U1. This boat operated off Stavanger, Norway, during the German invasion of that country, and was subsequently relegated to training duties.

Left: The original caption of this photograph states that these are watch officers aboard a German submarine, but the fact that they do not appear particularly watchful suggests that this photograph was taken during an off-duty period in port.

Above: German Type XXI submarines under construction at the Deschimag shipyard, Bremen. Some 40 U-boats were found here by the Allies in various stages of completion at the end of the war. Bremen was a frequent target for Allied bombing raids.

Left: The after section of a Seehund (Seal) two-man midget submarine. These craft were used mainly against Allied invasion forces. One torpedo was carried on each side, and the fuel tank was positioned underneath.

On 3 September, just hours after the declaration of war, the U-boat campaign in the Atlantic began with a tragedy for Britain when the commander of the *U30,* Lieutenant Lemp, torpedoed and sank the British passenger liner *Athenia* south of the Rockall Bank, mistaking the vessel for an armed merchant cruiser. About 1,300 survivors were rescued, but 112 people lost their lives. The incident led the British to believe that the Germans had initiated unrestricted submarine warfare; the truth was that the *Kriegsmarine,* for the time being at least, imposed even tighter restrictions on its U-boat commanders in an attempt to avoid the occurrence of similar accidents.

Below: The British aircraft carrier HMS Courageous sinking in the Western Approaches after being torpedoed by the U29 (Kapitanleutnant Schuhart) on 17 September 1939. After this loss, the Royal Navy withdrew its precious carriers from anti-submarine patrol work.

Early successes

In the first month of the war, the U-boats sank 30 merchant ships, either by mines or torpedo attack; the aircraft carrier *Ark Royal* also had a narrow escape off the Hebrides when a salvo of torpedoes launched by the *U39* detonated prematurely. On 17 September, however, Lieutenant Commander Schuhart's *U29* torpedoed and sank the carrier *Courageous* in the Western Approaches, with the loss of 515 lives. The Germans lost one U-boat during this period: the *U27*, sunk by British destroyers off the west coast of Scotland.

Submarine losses began to mount in October 1939, when three out of a tactical group of six U-boats – the forerunner of the 'wolfpacks' which would soon be deployed to the Atlantic area – were lost en route to their stations. The *U40* fell victim to a mine, while

Below: A Type XXI U-boat under construction at the Deschimag shipyard, Bremen, at the end of World War II. The first Type XXI (U2511) became operational in March 1945, but the class entered service too late to have any influence on the war at sea.

the *U42* and *U45* were sunk by convoy escorts. The remaining three boats, however, went on to sink 15 merchant ships before their patrol ended. The *U12* and *U16* were also sunk by mines in the English Channel during October, after which the German submarines were forbidden to use this dangerous stretch of water.

On the night of 13/14 October, in an operation conducted with great skill and daring, the German submarine *U47*, commanded by Lieutenant Commander Gunther Prien, penetrated the defences of Scapa Flow and sank the 27,500-ton battleship *Royal Oak*, a veteran of World War I, with three torpedo hits. The battleship went down with the loss of 833 lives. Prien was the first of the U-boat 'aces'; he was to lose his own life in March 1941, when *U47* fell victim to a depth-charge attack.

Top left: *The long-range Type IXD2 submarine* U873 *picture in dry dock at Portsmouth Navy Yard, New Hampshire, on 30 June 1945, after its surrender on 16 May. The Type IX was used for operations in distant waters, such as the Indian Ocean, and for transporting war materials to Germany's ally, Japan.*

Bottom left: *Construction work in progress on a U-boat base on the French Atlantic coast. At one stage, in late 1940, the Italians had more submarines operating in the Atlantic than the Germans, having deployed some of their craft to the French Atlantic ports.*

Below: *Inside a German submarine pen on the Atlantic coast, 1941. U-boat pens were heavily reinforced and were proof against all Allied bombs until the advent of the RAF's six-ton, deep penetration 'Tallboy' in 1944.*

Above: *A prefabricated U-boat hull section awaiting assembly at Bremen. As the war progressed, submarine production facilities were subjected to increasingly heavy air attack, but it was a combination of air with naval power that finally defeated the U-boats.*

Above: The U25, *seen here was a Type IA. In January and February 1940, under Commander Schütze, she sank six Allied ships totalling 27,335 tons, but was herself mined and sunk off Terschelling on 8 August the same year.*

Below left: Kapitanleutnant Günther Prien, whose U47 *sank the British battleship* Royal Oak *in Scapa Flow on 14 October 1939, with the loss of over 800 lives. Prien went on to sink 27 ships before he was lost in 1941.*

Below right: The return of the U47 *to Germany on 25 October 1939, following the daring and successful attack on the* Royal Oak. *Prien and his men were fêted as national heroes.*

In the seven months from September 1939 to March 1940, the U-boats sank 222 merchant ships totalling 764,766 tons, losing 18 of their number in the process. The submarine construction programme could not yet cope with this rate of attrition, and at the beginning of the Norwegian campaign in April 1940, only 31 U-boats were available for operations, divided into nine groups spread out in an arc from the Norwegian coast to the Shetland Islands. The Norwegian campaign, which ended in June 1940 with the evacuation of the Allied Expeditionary Force, cost the Germans five U-boats; fortunately for the Allies, the enemy submarine force had never been able to operate at peak efficiency due to a variety of technical problems, not least of which concerned the torpedoes, which continually malfunctioned.

Above: Oberleutnant zur Zee Endress, the man who fired the torpedo that sank the Royal Oak. *He went on to command, the* U46, *which survived the war. The loss of the* Royal Oak, *which had fought at Jutland, came as a profound shock for the Royal Navy.*

Above: Günther Prien (centre front) and the crew of the U47. *The* U47 *was depth-charged and sunk on the night of 7/8 March 1941 by the destroyer HMS* Wolverine. *Prien had been attempting to attack a convoy in the North Atlantic.*

Above: This photograph of Günther Prien was taken on 3 August 1940, following his return from another successful patrol. He is talking to three German airmen, picked up by the U47. Their flying boat had been shot down over the Atlantic.

Below: Crewmen keep watch from the conning tower of a Type IX U-boat in the North Atlantic, September 1942. A surfaced U-boat was extremely difficult to spot from warships escorting a convoy, which is why air cover proved invaluable to the Allies.

Wolfpacks in the Atlantic

The capture of the French Atlantic ports, following the collapse of France in the summer of 1940, gave the U-boats a tremendous tactical advantage. They could now proceed directly to their Atlantic patrol areas via the Bay of Biscay, and they were able to operate more closely in conjunction with Focke-Wulf FW200 maritime reconnaissance aircraft, operating from bases on the Atlantic coast. Even before the Atlantic bases were secured, the U-boats were meeting with growing success; in June 1940, they sank 58 ships amounting to nearly 300,000 tons, their biggest triumph to date.

Most of the U-boat attacks were made at night and on the surface, the submarines operating in packs of four or more. If one boat came into contact with a convoy, it would quickly summon the others, and an attack would be initiated once they were in position. This method produced considerable success, despite the fact that in the latter half of 1940, the Germans never had more than 15 U-boats on station at any one time. Until early 1941, in

Above: A U-boat takes on torpedoes during replenishment at sea. One by one, the German supply ships were hunted down, making the U-boats reliant on the large 'Milchkuh' submarines for replenishment. These, too, were all eventually sunk.

Below: Diet was always a problem for the U-boat crews. It consisted mainly of tinned food, seen here being loaded aboard U123. *This boat was one of the few to survive the war, and was ceded to France where she served as the* Blaison.

Above: The forward torpedo tubes of the U505. *This boat was forced to the surface by depth charges from the escort destroyer* USS Chatelain *on 1 June 1944, and was brought to Bermuda by a boarding party on the 19th with important naval codes.*

fact, more Italian submarines than German U-boats were operating in the Atlantic, the Italians having deployed some of their boats to the French Atlantic ports following their country's entry into the war in June 1940. Yet even with their depleted resources, the Germans were able to inflict massive losses on the Allied convoys; between 18 and 20 October 1940, for example, convoys SC7 and HX71 lost 31 ships between them to U-boat attacks.

The replacement of submarine losses – the total had reached 31 by March 1941 – continued to be a problem for the Germans, and there were delays in the operational deployment of those that were coming off the slipways. One reason for this was the thorough way in which U-boat crews were trained; it took nine months to bring a submarine crew to operational standard, a period during which it had to execute 66 simulated attacks in the Baltic Training Area. The upshot was that, at the end of 1940, the Germans were still only able to deploy 22 U-boats at once.

Nevertheless, the U-boat campaign brought Britain to the brink of starvation in the closing weeks of 1940. At the end of the year, food stocks had sunk to a perilously low level. Unless

Left: The aft torpedo room of the U505. This photograph gives a good idea of the cramped, stifling and unhygienic conditions in which U-boat crews were forced to live for weeks at a time.

Above: The crew of a Type VII U-boat enjoy a meal in the open air before spending the next few weeks in the metal confines of their submarine on an operational patrol.

Above: Even the captain's cabin on a U-boat was spartan, with wet clothing and towels draped everywhere. The bunk was fitted with restraining straps to keep the occupant secure. It was only the captain who was able to enjoy any degree of privacy.

Right: This U-boat has crash-dived following an aircraft alert. The helmsman takes evasive action according to the captain's instructions. From mid-1942, the threat from very long range patrol aircraft was ever present.

merchant ship sinkings could be reduced, Britain would starve before new merchant vessels could be built fast enough to maintain imports at the level needed for her survival.

The Allies break the 'Enigma'

Fortunately, the tonnage of merchant ships being sunk by U-boats fell dramatically in the second half of 1941, partly because more escort vessels were now available, enabling convoys to be escorted all the way across the Atlantic by British and Canadian warships, and partly thanks to a notable intelligence breakthrough that resulted following the capture of code books and an Enigma cypher machine from a German submarine, the *U110*, in May 1941. Within weeks, codebreakers at the highly secret Bletchley Park station had decyphered the German naval codes, and were consequently able to inform the Admiralty of the U-boats'

Above: A civilian hydrographer at work. He is drawing a new chart based on an old one of 1906. When Germany went to war in 1939 most charts pre-dated the previous conflict, and updating them was a huge task, which required a large civilian staff.

Below: The chart store at a German U-boat base. Carefully filed, these charts await distribution to U-boats departing on operational voyages. Charts, particularly of shallow water areas and the ocean floor, were clearly of enormous importance to underwater craft.

deployments. The result was dramatic. Thanks to the evasive routing of convoys, sinkings dropped from 300,000 tons in May and June 1941 to 100,000 tons in July and August, and in November, by which time the Germans had 80 U-boats at sea, the sinkings dropped to 62,000 tons, the lowest figure for 18 months.

The U-boats in the Mediterranean

In the autumn of 1941, U-boats were deployed to the Mediterranean for the first time, their principal task being to attack Malta's supply lines. The island of Malta, under siege since June 1940, was a thorn in the Axis flesh, a formidable base from which British warships and strike aircraft made continual attacks on enemy convoys carrying reinforcements and equipment to North Africa. The new arrivals scored an early success when, on 13 November 1941, the aircraft carrier *Ark Royal*, homeward bound

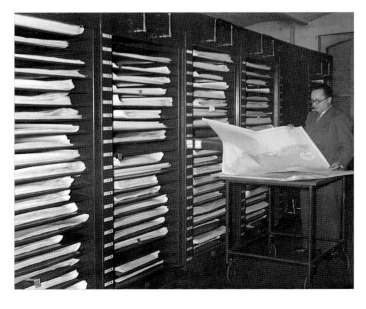

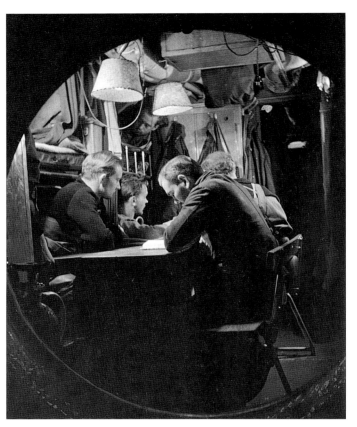

for Gibraltar after flying off fighters to Malta, was hit near her starboard boiler room by one of a salvo of four torpedoes fired by the German submarine *U81*. Only one crew member lost his life in the attack and valiant efforts were made to save the carrier, but she sank under tow only 46km (25nm) from Gibraltar.

Less than a fortnight later, on 25 November, the battleship HMS *Barham*, which had set out from Alexandria with other warships to intercept an Italian convoy, was torpedoed by the *U331*, capsized and exploded with the loss of 861 men; there were 450 survivors. Then, on the night of 14/15 December, the *U557* sank the cruiser *Galatea* off Alexandria, and four days later the cruiser *Neptune* and the destroyer *Kandahar* were sunk by mines, the former with the loss of all but one of her 550 crew.

At the end of the year, the German submarines in the Mediterranean were heavily reinforced, so that early in 1942, the number of boats in the theatre had risen to 21 vessels. The main target of the U-boat fleet in the Mediterranean was now the tankers plying

Left: Off duty, there was little for a U-boat crew to do but read, sleep, play chess, or listen to gramaphone records. Life aboard a submarine was incredibly stressful, but a submerged submarine could be a tolerably comfortable environment when it was not under attack.

Left: *The Grand Harbour, Malta, seen under heavy air attack by the Luftwaffe. Allied convoys to the besieged island were an important target for the U-boats. In turn, attacks on Axis supply lines by British aircraft and submarines from the island, played a key part in the defeat of Rommel's forces in North Africa.*

Above: *The pilot of a Neger 'human torpedo' full of smiles after a successful mission. The smile is probably one of relief. The transparent dome that covered his head and shoulders could only be unfastened and removed from the outside. The Negers attacked the Allied invasion forces at Normandy, but suffered heavy losses.*

Top left: Pictured over the starboard wing of a Blohm und Voss BV138 reconnaissance aircraft, are the ships of the ill-fated Russian convoy PQ17 in July 1942. In fear of the presence of German warships, the convoy was misguidedly ordered to scatter. Twenty-eight ships were sunk by German aircraft and U-boats.

Bottom left: The end of a merchantmen in the Mediterranean, 1942. The Germans deployed increasing numbers of U-boats to this theatre of the war. The relatively shallow waters were not ideal for the operation of large ocean-going submarines.

between Egypt and the vital oil ports in the Levant, but the cost to the Germans was heavy; between January and June 1942, eight U-boats were sunk, together with 10 Italian boats.

The Arctic theatre

In 1942, the German U-boat arm extended its operations to the Arctic, where its task was to attack the Allied convoys transporting supplies to the Soviet Union, invaded by the Germans in June 1941. A U-boat group, code-named Ulan, was deployed to northern waters at the end of December 1941, establishing a patrol area south of Bear Island, between Spitzbergen and northern Norway. During the months that followed, the U-boats operated intensively against the Arctic convoys with varying success, their efforts often thwarted by bad weather, and in June 1942, in a series of attacks on the scattered Convoy PQ17, they sank nine merchantmen and finished off seven more that had been damaged earlier by air attack.

Easy pickings

Meanwhile, early in January 1942, 12 Type VII-C U-boats had been deployed to operate in the area of the Newfoundland Bank. Between them, from 8 January to 12 February, they sank 21 ships. At the same time, Admiral Dönitz authorized the beginning of Operation *Paukenschlag* (Drumbeat), a U-boat offensive against American mercantile traffic in the western Atlantic. The Americans had not yet adopted a convoy system, and between 11 January and 7 February 1942 a mere five U-boats sank 26 ships, all of which were sailing independently, and damaged several more. A second wave of five Type IX U-boats, operating off the US eastern seaboard between 21 January and 6 March, sank a further 19 vessels, while off Canada another eight Type VII craft sank nine more, together with the destroyer HMS *Belmont*. After May 1942, when the Americans finally established a convoy system, the U-boats switched their area of operations to the Gulf of Mexico and the Caribbean, where they operated with success for some three months, until a convoy system was established in these waters too.

The achievement of the German U-boats in the first half of 1942 was little short of staggering. In all waters, they had sunk 585 merchantmen totalling more than 3,000,000 tons for the loss of 21 submarines. One hundred new boats were either in service or under construction. By the end of the year, the picture that con-

Above: The prototype Enigma code-machine, first developed by Dr Arthur Scherbius in 1923. The possession by British intelligence of the Enigma naval code played a significant, if not decisive, part in winning the Battle of the Atlantic, and also in the defeat of the Italian Navy in the Mediterranean.

fronted the Allies was even gloomier; the number of Allied merchant ships sunk during 1942 had risen to 1,664, totalling some 8,000,000 tons, out of a total of 3862 sunk since the war began in September 1939; U-boat losses during that period came to 152, a profitable exchange rate. There was now a serious danger that the rate of sinkings would outstrip the rate of Allied merchant ship construction; if this happened, the consequences for Britain's imports, already reduced to two-thirds their 1939 level, would be catastrophic.

A major part of the problem confronting the Allies was that, in February 1942, the Germans had introduced a new code called

Above: The famous Captain F. J. Walker, Commander of the 2nd Escort Group, aboard the sloop HMS Starling. Walker died suddenly in July 1944, probably as a result of the immense strain of nearly five years of almost continuous anti-submarine operations.

Triton, intended solely for use with U-boats in the Atlantic. It confounded the codebreakers for 10 months until, by an incredible stroke of luck, documents recovered from a U-boat sunk in the Mediterranean in December 1942 at last enabled the experts to break it. The resulting intelligence revealed that 100 U-boats were operationally deployed, 50 of them in the Atlantic. Of these, 37 were in the so-called 'air gap' south of Greenland, the mid-ocean area that was beyond the radius of action of maritime patrol aircraft.

The breaking of the Triton cypher meant that the Allies were once again able to re-route their convoys and avoid the U-boat concentrations; sinkings dropped off dramatically during the early weeks of 1943. Nevertheless, from 3–12 January, the U-boats scored a notable success by sinking seven out of nine tankers in Convoy TM1, sailing from Trinidad to Gibraltar, and in February Admiral Dönitz – whose intelligence service had decrypted the Allied cyphers that controlled the movements of the convoys – launched a renewed onslaught, his submarines attacking in packs of up to 20 boats. In the North Atlantic, two such wolfpacks sank 27 ships of 103 that sailed in two convoys, while in the central Atlantic, U-boats replenishing from Type IX 'Milchkuh' supply submarines sank 36 more before the month ended.

These losses were bad enough, but there was worse to come. In March, the cypher experts lost their grip on Triton for a fortnight, with the result that this month became the worst ever for convoy

Left: A depth-charge attack in progress, seen from the sloop Starling of the 2nd Escort Group. These hunter-killer groups, operating in conjunction with aircraft, eventually got the better of the U-boats.

Above: *A Walter-type U-boat seen during trials at Hamburg in 1944. Powered by a thermal fuel, high-test peroxide, a few Type XVIIB Walter boat prototypes were ready by the end of the war. However, the propulsion system was unreliable.*

Below: *Icy conditions aboard a U-boat in northern waters in 1942. In the beginning the waters between North Cape and Spitzbergen were a killing ground for U-boats, and the Soviets did little to help in the way of providing escort forces.*

Right: U-boat pens at Le Havre after an attack by RAF Lancasters armed with six-ton deep-penetration 'Tallboy' bombs. Until the advent of these weapons in 1944, the U-boats were completely safe inside these massively reinforced structures.

Far right: Submarine pens at Lorient under attack by B-17 Flying Fortresses of the USAAF's 8th Bomber Command, 21 October 1942. Although the B-17s were able to bomb very accurately from high altitude, their bombs made little impression on their targets.

sinkings. In all waters, the U-boats sank 108 ships totalling 627,000 tons. It was the closest the German submarines ever came to severing the transatlantic sea links between the old world and the new.

A reversal of fortune

But the tide was about to turn. In March, as the Atlantic battles raged, representatives of the British, American and Canadian navies met in an 'Atlantic Convoy Conference' in Washington. It was agreed that the US Navy should assume responsibility for the tanker convoys running between Britain and the West Indies, leaving the North Atlantic entirely to the British and Canadians. The Royal Canadian Navy, directed by a new North-West Atlantic Command HQ at Halifax, would be entirely responsible for the North Atlantic convoys as far as 47 degrees west, where the Royal Navy would take over. March also saw the formation of the first Support Groups, which would provide rapid reinforcement for convoys under threat; two of the first five were composed of

destroyers drawn from the Home Fleet, two of escort vessels from the Western Approaches Command, all with highly experienced crews, and the fifth was formed around the escort carrier HMS *Biter*.

The reorganization of the escort forces produced immediate results. In three months to the end of May 1943, the Allies sank 56 U-boats, 41 in May alone. This was five more than the number of boats that actually left port, so that for the first time there was a decrease in the number of U-boats on offensive patrol. It brought the number sunk between the beginning of 1943 and the end of May to 96, of which 52 were sunk by aircraft. This last fact was significant, for the mid-Atlantic gap was slowly but surely being closed. The maritime patrol aircraft that had borne the brunt of anti-submarine work since the beginning of the war – Hudsons, Catalinas and Sunderlands – were now joined in growing numbers by very long range B-17 Fortresses and B-24 Liberators, equipped with more efficient ASV (Air to Surface Vessel) radar and other detection devices, while Wellingtons fitted with

searchlights prowled the Bay of Biscay at night to catch submarines in transit to and from their home bases. In this task they were aided by Dönitz himself, who had issued an order that U-boats were to traverse the Bay of Biscay on the surface by both day and night, relying on their AA armament to fight off Allied aircraft. This order remained in force for some three months, from May to August 1943, and in that time the Germans lost 28 U-boats to air attack in the Bay. The cost to the Allies was 57 aircraft.

Compounding Dönitz's problems was the fact that his vital supply submarines, of which there were only 10, were being picked off one by one. Also, from February 1943, groups of long-range Type IX U-boats, which might have been profitably employed in the Atlantic, were deployed to the Indian Ocean, where they continued to operate until early 1945 with limited success, using Japanese bases on the Malay Peninsula.

Withdrawal from the Atlantic

September 1943 saw the start of a renewed offensive against the Atlantic convoys, the U-boats now being equipped with search receiver equipment, eight 20mm anti-aircraft guns and a new acoustic homing torpedo, the T5 *Zaunkonig* (Wren). The submarines were deployed in attack waves of up to 20 boats, but their efforts were frustrated by strong Allied naval support groups comprising destroyers, corvettes and frigates, by the constant presence of long-range aircraft and, by no means least important, by the regular malfunction of their own T5 torpedoes, many of which failed to explode or detonated prematurely in the wake of the target vessel.

In all, Dönitz lost 25 U-boats in the Atlantic during September and October 1943, and they achieved nothing more than the sinking of nine merchant ships out of the 2,468 convoyed across the ocean. This was an unacceptably poor exchange rate. Vigorous action by Allied air and surface forces, together with evasive routing, compelled Dönitz to abandon his wolfpack tactics in November 1943 and to withdraw all but a few boats from the North Atlantic, where they continued for months to hunt for convoys with negligible success. The main U-boat forces were sent to operate against the Gibraltar convoys, where they had the advantage of

Left: Schnorchel equipment aboard the U3008. This Type XXI boat was surrendered at Kiel in May 1945, and was used for trials by the United States Navy. It was finally scrapped in 1949.

Top left: *A U-boat* schnorchel *fitted with the electro-magnetic head valve under development at the end of World War II. The valve is covered with anti-radar matting; the cage at the top is the GSR, a radar detection dipole.*

Above: *A Type XVIIB U-boat being lifted by a floating crane at Cuxhaven on 11 August 1945. The boat is probably either the U1406 or U1407, both of which were scuttled. The U1407 served with the RN as a trials craft and was scrapped in 1950.*

Above: *The periscope of a German Biber (Beaver) midget submarine, cleverly camouflaged for an attack on the bridge at Nijmegen, captured by American airborne forces in September 1944.*

Right: *A U-boat under attack by a Short Sunderland flying boat of RAF Coastal Command. Effective though it was, the Sunderland did not have sufficient range to cover the so-called mid-Atlantic gap, where convoys were vulnerable.*

air support, and during the ensuing months, many battles were fought in Iberian waters and the south-western approaches.

From January to March 1944, only three merchant ships were sunk out of 3,360 convoyed, and in the whole of 1944, 36 were sunk. Two major factors contributed to the Germans' lack of success. The first was Allied air power; with escort carriers now a regular feature of the Atlantic convoys, joining the long-range maritime aircraft in the battle against the U-boats, submarine losses to air attack in the Atlantic now exceeded those in the Biscay area. The second factor was the growing expertise of the Allied naval hunter-killer groups, whose warships were now armed with a formidable array of anti-submarine weaponry that included forward-mounted rocket launchers, capable of hurling a pattern of depth charges ahead of a vessel to ensnare the U-boat it was pursuing.

Such was the background to the successful transport of US forces to Britain, making it possible to launch the Normandy invasion on time.

New technology arrives too late

The introduction of new devices such as the *Schnorchel* apparatus, which enabled U-boats to remain submerged without the need to surface to recharge their systems, did nothing to solve the Germans' problems. When the Allied invasion came, only the *Schnorchel*-equipped boats were able to approach the invasion area.

Above: Checking torpedoes before loading in a German storage facility on the French Atlantic coast, in May 1943. The predicament of the still-tenacious U-boat crews was not helped by the fact that, on the increasingly rare occasions when they did manage to engage an enemy vessel, their torpedoes regularly malfunctioned, thus wasting a valuable opportunity to regain the offensive. By this time the Allies were winning the Battle of the Atlantic, and U-boat losses were outstripping production.

Above: A Bristol Beaufighter of the Balkan Air Force makes a rocket attack on the hiding place of small surface and submersible craft in the northern Adriatic. The submersibles were concealed between the shore and a wrecked ship.

Right: A Leigh Light installation on a Vickers Wellington bomber of Coastal Command. These powerful searchlights were used to illuminate U-boats attempting to cross the Bay of Biscay under cover of darkness. Even surfaced U-boats could be very difficult to spot.

The non-*Schnorchel* boats that tried to approach were subjected to heavy air attack, and either sunk or forced to withdraw in the face of overwhelming opposition. Even the *Schnorchel*-equipped boats, which were able to evade air attack, did not succeed in penetrating the invasion area until some two weeks after D-Day, and they enjoyed only limited success.

In the Arctic too, the escort forces had gained the upper hand. In late March and early April 1944, for example, 17 U-boats made repeated attacks on Convoy JW58 and were completely unsuccessful, losing four of their number in the process.

Overall, losses became increasingly grievous, until they reached the point later in the year when almost one submarine was being destroyed for every Allied ship sunk.

During the winter of 1944–45, the *Schnorchel* U-boats launched their final offensive against Allied shipping in the Atlantic and in British home waters; however, the British air and surface anti-submarine forces inflicted such heavy losses on the U-boats that they were forced out of the coastal waters. Between 15 November 1944 and 27 January 1945, the U-boats sank 31 ships, including some naval escort vessels, but they also lost 12 of their number. At the end of January, a new class of U-boat, the Type XXIII, became operational, and in the following five-week period, they sank 16 ships and damaged several others; but 10 more U-boats fell victim to the anti-submarine forces.

The Type XXIII was one of two types of submarine on which Admiral Dönitz had pinned great hopes. Designed for operations in coastal waters, it was very quiet, displaced 256 tons, was 34m (112ft)

Below: Officers of the Royal Navy inspect a **Delphin (Dolphin)** *two-man midget submarine, captured at the end of World War II. Only two prototypes were completed, and no particulars of their armament were ever released.*

in length, and carried a 14-man crew. A much larger variant was the Type XXI; displacing 1,652 tons submerged, it was an ocean-going craft capable of fully submerged operations using *Schnorchel* and conventional diesel-electric drive. Its submerged speed was 30km/h (16 knots), and it was armed with 23 torpedoes. For speed of building, it was constructed in prefabricated sections. Admiral Dönitz planned to renew operations against the Allied convoys with the Type XXI late in 1944, but construction was frustrated by the Allied bombing campaign and it never became operational.

The bitter end

The surviving U-boats fought on to the last. In April 1945, they launched their last operation in British coastal waters, sinking eight ships but losing 15 of their number. The last U-boat to be destroyed in World War II was the *U320*, sunk off Bergen by a Catalina of No 210 Squadron RAF on 7 May, 1945.

Of the 1162 U-boats built and commissioned during World War II, 785 were lost through various causes, leaving 156 to be surrendered to the Allies, and the rest to be scuttled at the end of the

war. Surface ships accounted for 246 U-boats, shore-based maritime patrol aircraft destroyed 245, and shipborne aircraft 43. The destruction of another 50 submarines was shared between surface ships and aircraft, while Allied submarines accounted for 21. The rest were destroyed by mines, bombing raids and accidents, or – in the case of 29 boats – lost without trace.

The lion's share of the destruction was attributed to the British and Commonwealth forces, which sank 514 U-boats. United States forces sank 166; a further 12 were shared between British and US forces.

Of the 40,000 German submariners who went to sea in World War II, 30,000 never returned. It was a casualty figure that almost exactly matched that of the British Merchant Navy alone.

Above: Surrendered German U-boats in Wilhelmshaven at the end of the war, prior to being handed over to the Allies. Most of the survivors of Dönitz's once-proud fleet were scuttled in the North Atlantic by the Royal Navy.

Right: Surrendered German U-boats at Lisahally near Londonderry, Northern Ireland. The last operational U-boats were not transferred from Wilhelmshaven to Britain until the last week of June, 1945.

Below: Crowds line the river banks to watch the Type VIIC U-boat U776 arriving at Westminster Pier on the River Thames, where the boat was opened for public inspection.

CHAPTER 3

COMMERCE RAIDERS

The aim of the *Kriegsmarine* on the outbreak of war was to destroy the Allied merchant fleets, using a combination of 'pocket battleships', battlecruisers and armed merchant cruisers. The task of the Allies was to hunt them down.

The deployment of U-boats to their war stations in August 1939 was closely followed by that of two of the *Kriegsmarine*'s 'pocket battleships', the *Admiral Graf Spee* and the *Deutschland*, which sailed from Wilhelmshaven on 21 and 24 August respectively. While the *Graf Spee* headed for the South Atlantic, the *Deutschland* sailed for a position to the south of Greenland. Both warships were preceded by their supply and support vessels, the fleet tankers *Altmark* and *Westerwald*.

It was not until 26 September, nearly four weeks after the outbreak of war, that the German Naval High Command issued orders permitting the two warships to begin offensive operations against British and French merchant shipping. By this time, the *Deutschland* had moved south to cover the Bermuda-Azores shipping route, where she claimed her first victim on 30 September. The *Graf Spee* also sank her first merchantman, the British steamer *Clement*, off Pernambuco on 30 September, and between 5 and 12 October she sank four more before breaking off to replenish from her supply ship. There was no further news of her until 2 December, when she sank the freighters *Doric Star* and *Tairoa* between St Helena and South Africa. The *Deutschland*, meanwhile, had moved

Left: An aerial view of the **Panzerschiff** *(armoured ship)* **Admiral Graf Spee.** *This photograph was taken in August 1939, shortly before she deployed to the South Atlantic to start her commerce raiding career – a career that was to end ignominiously at Montevideo.*

Right: The 'pocket battleship' **Deutschland** *on a visit to Swinemünde in May 1937. She was later renamed* **Lützow,** *and saw most of her war service in Arctic waters, taking part in the Battle of the Barents Sea. She subsequently served with the Baltic Training Squadron, and by the end of her career had sunk 6962 tons of shipping.*

Above: *The* Admiral Graf Spee *seen at Spithead in 1937 on the occasion of the naval review in celebration of the coronation of King George VI. The* Graf Spee *was commissioned as fleet flagship in 1936.*

Below: Admiral Scheer *(foreground) and* Deutschland *at Swinemünde in May 1937 when, while blockading Spanish ports,* Deutschland *was bombed and damaged by Spanish Republican aircraft. The* Scheer *bombarded Almeria in retaliation.*

into the North Atlantic, where she operated with limited success until being recalled to Germany early in November.

The Battle of the River Plate

It was not until late September that Allied naval intelligence knew for certain that the German warships were at sea, but as soon as the fact was established, a massive search for them was mounted by British and French naval forces. Before the outbreak of war, the Admiralty, in conjunction with the French Navy, had formed eight Atlantic battle groups of aircraft carriers and cruisers for the defence of merchant shipping against surface raiders; one of these, known as Group G, was responsible for the waters off the east coast of South America, and was consequently well-placed to intercept the

Below: On 18 April 1939, major units of the German fleet took part in a month-long training voyage, in effect a dress rehearsal for their deployments at the start of World War II. Seen here are the Admiral Graf Spee *and the* Deutschland.

Left: The British heavy cruiser Exeter *seen on a visit to New York in 1939.* Exeter *was launched in July 1929 and mounted six 8in (203mm) guns; During the Battle of the River Plate she was hit by seven 11in (280mm) shells, and was put out of action with no 8in (203mm) guns able to fire. She underwent a refit and deployed to the Eastern Fleet some 14 months later.*

Top left: The tanker Altmark *was assigned to the* Admiral Graf Spee *as its supply ship. Commanded by Captain Dau, she sailed for the USA on 5 August 1939 to take on fuel oil before heading for her first rendezvous with the pocket battleship. After the Battle of the River Plate,* Altmark *managed to evade all the British ships seeking her, and returned safely to Norwegian waters.*

Bottom left: Captain Hans Langsdorff confers with Argentinian officials in Uruguay after his ship had sailed out into Montevideo. His crew was interned in Argentina for the duration of the war after the Graf Spee *was scuttled.*

Right: Commodore (later Admiral Sir) Henry Harwood, the senior officer of the British warship group that hunted down the Graf Spee. *Harwood later became C-in-C Mediterranean Fleet.*

Graf Spee. This battle group comprised the heavy cruisers *Exeter* and *Cumberland*, and could be quickly reinforced by the light cruisers *Ajax* and *Achilles*, the latter belonging to the Royal New Zealand Navy. The senior officer of Group G, Commodore Henry Harwood, shrewdly reasoned that Hans Langsdorff, captain of the *Graf Spee*, would make for the waters off the River Plate – the waterway separating Uruguay from Argentina – his main hunting ground, as British and French mercantile traffic could always be found there in considerable numbers. Detaching HMS *Cumberland* to cover the Falkland Islands, he ordered his warships (now designated Force G) to set up patrol lines in that area of ocean.

Two more battle groups were also ordered to take part in the search. Force H, with the cruisers *Shropshire* and *Sussex*, was to

proceed to the area between Cape Town and St Helena, while Force K, which comprised the battlecruiser *Renown*, the aircraft carrier *Ark Royal* and the cruiser *Neptune*, was dispatched to search along a line from Freetown to the Central South Atlantic. Harwood's guesswork soon paid dividends. At 0608 on 13 December, the three British cruisers sighted the *Graf Spee* heading for the Plate estuary and closed in to attack her from different directions in order to divide the firepower of her 280mm (11in) main armament. After a while, however, Langsdorff concentrated his fire on the *Exeter*, his shells inflicting heavy damage on the cruiser. Despite this, *Exeter*'s captain, F.S. Bell, continued to engage the enemy throughout the night. By daybreak, *Exeter* was ablaze, with only one gun turret still in action. Only when the *Graf Spee* made smoke and turned away did Bell break off the action and retire to the south-east, with 61 of his crew dead and 23 wounded.

Top left: The communications room on the **Admiral Graf Spee.** *It was from here that Langsdorff sent his final messages to Berlin, and here that the instruction to scuttle his ship was received from German naval headquarters. It was the humiliating circumstances of the loss of the* Graf Spee *which prompted Hitler to rename the* Deutschland, Lützow, *to avoid any possibility of a ship bearing the name of the Fatherland being sunk.*

Bottom left: Captain Hans Langsdorff shares a joke with members of his crew in happier times. During her raiding operations in the Atlantic, the warship sank nine merchant vessels totalling 50,089 tons. Langsdorff was extremely courteous to captured merchant seamen.

Right: A close-up view of starboard side of the Graf Spee's conning tower, showing the large optical rangefinder at the top and an array of radio aerials. One of the warship's 5.9in (150mm) guns can be seen at the bottom of the picture. It is also possible to discern the disruptive pattern of her camouflage on the superstructure, which, along with the false bow wave and wash – the camouflage she had at the River Plate – appear to have been the idea of her captain.

Above: *The final minutes of the* Admiral Graf Spee. *A huge column of smoke rises from the stricken warship, while a tug stands by to carry out a rescue mission in case anyone has been left on board the vessel.*

Right: *The wreck of the* Graf Spee *was photographed on 2 February 1940 by Ensign Sampson of the US Navy from the cruiser USS* Helena. *Sampson also made a sketch showing the German warship's salient points, such as the rangefinder. The hulk was broken up in situ in 1942.*

Above: The scuttled wreck of the Graf Spee *burned for a week and drew crowds of sightseers. Captain Langsdorff, a most honourable officer, accepted all the blame for the demise of his ship and committed suicide, an action regretted by many of his colleagues.*

Ajax and *Achilles* continued to engage the *Graf Spee* as the latter steered for the coast of Uruguay. A heavy hit put both of *Ajax*'s after turrets out of action and the German warship continued to fire salvoes at her pursuers until she entered the estuary, whereupon Commodore Harcourt withdrew his ships to watch and wait. He was aware that his cruisers, outgunned and with their armament reduced through battle damage, were in grave danger of being overwhelmed by the *Graf Spee* should Langsdorff choose to fight his way out.

The end of the Graf Spee

But the *Graf Spee* was damaged, too. She had taken some 70 shell hits and 36 of her crew were dead, with another 60 wounded. She was also short of ammunition. Langsdorff had therefore decided to make for the neutral port of Montevideo, where the wounded could be taken off, and temporary repairs made to his ship before he attempted a breakout and return to Germany. It was estimated that the repairs would take two weeks. The *Graf Spee* could legally remain in a neutral port for only 72 hours. Such was Langsdorff's dilemma.

It was now, amid an intense flurry of diplomatic activity, that the art of deception came into its own. During the next few hours, the British Admiralty transmitted a series of signals on frequencies known to be monitored by the enemy. The signals indicated that reinforcement battle groups were descending on the Plate Estuary, ready to destroy the *Graf Spee* as soon as she emerged. In fact, only the cruiser HMS *Cumberland* was near enough to make an immediate impression; the nearest heavy naval units, the aircraft carrier *Ark Royal* and the battlecruiser *Renown*, were still 4630km (2500nm) away.

The British ruse worked. Langsdorff, convinced that a vastly superior British naval force was lying in wait for him, signalled Berlin and outlined his options. There were only two. Either he could try to break through to Buenos Aires, the capital of supposedly neutral Argentina, whose government was strongly sympathetic towards the Germans, and allow his ship to be interned; or he could take her out into the Plate estuary and scuttle her.

By nightfall on 17 December, it was apparent that the Uruguayan authorities were not prepared to allow the *Graf Spee* to remain in Montevideo beyond the 72-hour time limit. The decision was therefore taken to scuttle her. On the following morning, watched by a vast crowd of sightseers, *Graf Spee* put to sea. The British warships cleared for action, but before they could engage the enemy, their spotter aircraft reported that the *Graf Spee* had been scuttled and blown up by her own crew. Within a short time, it was learned that Captain Langsdorff had committed suicide.

Auxiliary commerce raiders

The *Graf Spee* was finished; but what she might have achieved was indicated by the fact that, in her brief career, she had destroyed nine ships totalling 50,089 tons. Luckily for the Allies, technical considerations had prevented the full deployment of the other two 'pocket battleships'. The *Deutschland* had to return to Germany for an overhaul after sinking only two ships (renamed *Lützow*, she would operate briefly against merchant shipping in the Skagerrak in the winter of 1939–40), and the third 'pocket battleship', the *Admiral Scheer*, was undergoing a refit at the outbreak of war. It would be October 1940 before she deployed to the high seas.

In March 1940, however, another serious threat to Allied commerce emerged with the sailing of the auxiliary cruiser *Atlantis*. She was a merchant ship – the *Goldenfels*, built originally for the Hansa

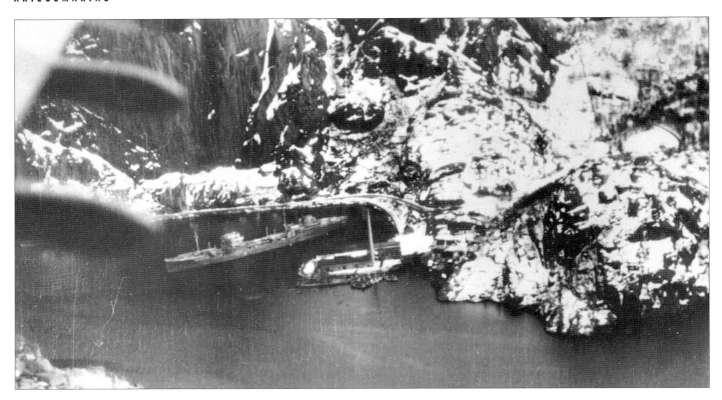

Above: The Graf Spee's replenishment tanker, Altmark, *in Jossing Fjord. On the night of 16 February 1940, she was boarded by the crew of the British destroyer* Cossack *who rescued British merchant seamen captured from ships sunk by the Graf Spee.*

Below: A formation of Heinkel He 114 floatplanes. This type, and the Arado Ar 196 monoplane equipped all major German surface units. They were used for gunnery spotting or reconnaissance. Bismarck *had provision for carrying six 'spotter' aircraft.*

*Above: Known to the British as 'Raider G', **Kormoran** sank or captured 11 ships totalling 68,274 tons, in a 350-day sortie. Powered by diesel-electric machinery she mounted a variety of armament: guns, torpedoes, mines, an MTB as well as two Ar 196A-1 floatplanes. She was eventually caught off Shark Bay, Western Australia, by the cruiser **Sydney**, on 11 November 1941, and after an exchange of gunfire, both vessels went down.*

Line – fitted with heavy concealed armament, so that she retained her merchant ship appearance. The Germans had used similar vessels with great success during World War I, and the success was to be repeated by this new generation. *Atlantis*, known as 'Raider C' to the British because she was the third to be identified, even though she had been the first to sail, displaced 7,862 tons and was armed with six 15cm (5.9in) and one 7.62cm (3in) guns, two 37mm and two 20mm AA guns, and four 53cm (21in) torpedo tubes. She also carried two Heinkel He 114 floatplanes. She could make 30km/h (16 knots) and her complement was 350.

By the end of 1940 six more were deployed: the *Orion*, *Widder* (Ram), *Thor*, *Pinguin*, *Komet*, and *Kormoran*. Replenishing from supply ships at secret ocean rendezvous points, they preyed only on solitary unescorted vessels sailing the world's oceans. The British Admiralty's answer to these commerce raiders was to launch a major search for them using Armed Merchant Cruisers, 15 of which had been converted from fast liners. They were unar-

moured and underarmed, and no match for their adversaries, a fact well illustrated when the AMC *Rawalpindi* was sent to the bottom in minutes by the battlecruiser *Scharnhorst* in November 1939.

Under the command of Captain Rogge, *Atlantis* set out for the South Atlantic in March 1940, laying minefields off the African coast as she went. In a voyage lasting 622 days, operating in the South Atlantic and the Indian Ocean, she sank 22 Allied ships totalling 145,697 tons. Her victims included the French passenger liner *Commissaire Ramel*, serving under the British flag, and the Egyptian passenger ship *Zamzam*, which proved to be carrying 138 American civilians. On one occasion, *Atlantis* had a lucky escape when she sailed within 7km (4nm) of the British battleship *Nelson* and the aircraft carrier *Ark Royal* at night without being detected.

Then, on 22 November 1941, as she was replenishing the German submarine *U126* north of Ascension Island, she was surprised by the British heavy cruiser *Devonshire* and forced to scuttle herself after being heavily shelled. Lieutenant Commander Bauer of the *U126*, having submerged nearby, waited until the cruiser had departed and then surfaced to take the lifeboats bearing *Atlantis*'s survivors in tow, handing them over to the submarine supply ship *Python* which was summoned to the scene. The latter was herself sunk by the cruiser *Dorsetshire* on 1 December, the survivors reaching home after a rescue operation by German and Italian submarines.

Above: A dramatic painting by Norman Wilkinson depicting the fatal encounter between the Scharnhorst *and the British armed merchant cruiser* Rawalpindi, *southeast of Iceland, on 23 November 1939. All 15 of the fast merchant ships converted to the armed cruiser role by the Allies at the beginning of the war were sunk.*

Left: Captain Eyssen, who commanded the very successful raider Komet, *was typical of the generally courageous and honourable commanders of the auxiliary raiders, and made all reasonable effort to rescue the crews of the ships which he sank.*

The next commerce raider to be deployed after *Atlantis*, on 6 April 1940, was Commander Weyher's *Orion*. June 1940 found her in New Zealand waters, where she sowed minefields before going on to sink seven ships. In November she was joined by Captain Eyssen's *Komet*; this vessel reached her operational area in the Pacific by way of the Siberian sea route, her passage assisted by Soviet icebreakers. *Orion* and *Komet* sank seven more ships between them before parting company; *Orion* reached Bordeaux in August 1941, sinking two more ships during her homeward passage, after a voyage that had lasted a total of 510 days. In 1942, she was turned into a floating workshop, and in 1944, renamed

Hektor, she became a gunnery training ship. She was bombed and sunk at Swinemünde on 4 May 1945.

Komet arrived back at Hamburg in November 1941, also after a 510-day voyage, having added three more ships to her score. On 7 October 1942, she sailed from Flushing on a second voyage, but a week later she was torpedoed and sunk off the Cap de la Hague, France, by the British motor torpedo boat *MTB236* with the loss of all on board.

Success with honour

The third raider to sail, Commander von Ruckteschell's *Widder* (Ram), set out on 6 May 1940 bound for the central Atlantic, where in a voyage of 179 days, she sank or captured 10 ships totalling 58,645 tons. From 1941, she was a floating workshop in Norwegian waters; in May 1945, she was seized by Britain, where she was renamed *Ulysses* until being returned to Germany in 1953 under the name *Fechenheim*. Von Ruckteschell stood out among the captains of the German auxiliary cruisers; they were largely

Left: *Captain Gümprich, the brilliantly successful skipper of the German auxiliary cruiser* Thor *(Schiff 10). In two voyages,* Thor *sank or captured 22 ships, including the armed merchant cruiser* Voltaire.

Below: *The battlecruiser* Scharnhorst *pictured at Wilhelmshaven.* Scharnhorst *and her sister ship* Gneisenau *presented a dire threat to Allied convoys, but early attempts to break out into the Atlantic were thwarted.*

honourable men who stayed well within the bounds of international law, and did their utmost to ensure the survival of the crews of the merchant vessels they destroyed. A ruthless man, whose code of conduct did not include giving merchant crews a chance to abandon their ships before he opened fire on them, von Ruckteschell was ultimately brought to trial as a war criminal.

Two raiders sailed in June 1940, the first being the *Thor* under Captain Kahler. Her operational area was also the Atlantic, where in a voyage of 329 days she sank or captured 12 ships totalling 96,547 tons, including the British armed merchant cruiser *Voltaire*. In November 1941, she set out on a second cruise, under the command of Captain Gümprich and bound for the Pacific. On this voyage she sank or captured 10 ships totalling 56,037 tons. On 30 November 1942, while at Yokohama, Japan, she was destroyed when the adjacent tanker *Uckermark* – formerly the *Altmark* – caught fire and blew up.

The other raider to sail in June, the *Pinguin* (Captain Krüder) was the most successful of all in terms of ships sunk, narrowly beating *Atlantis* to the highest tonnage. She operated in the Indian Ocean, where nine ships fell victim to the mines she had laid or to her gunfire, and then sailed for the Antarctic. Her mission there was to attack the Norwegian whaling fleet, whose ships had made for Allied ports when Norway was overrun by the Nazis. She was very successful, capturing two factory ships and 11 whalers, all but three of which were escorted to French Atlantic ports in March 1941 with 22,200 tons of whale oil on board.

In all, during her 321-day voyage, *Pinguin* was responsible for the destruction of 32 ships totalling 154,619 tons. Her destructive career was brought to an end on 8 May 1941, when she was intercepted off the Seychelles by the heavy cruiser HMS *Cornwall*, and sunk with the loss of 541 men – 200 of them sailors who had been taken prisoner when the raider sank their vessels. The *Cornwall* managed to rescue only three officers, 57 seamen and 22 prisoners.

A mutually fatal engagement

On 3 December 1940, another raider set out for the Atlantic and Indian Oceans. She was the *Kormoran* (Commodore Detmers), and in a spree lasting 352 days, she sank or captured 11 ships of 68,264 tons, before being intercepted by the Royal Australian Navy's light cruiser *Sydney* on 19 November 1941, about 315km (170nm) west of Shark Bay, Western Australia. The wily Captain Detmers lured the Australian cruiser to close range by prolonging the signal exchanges between the two ships, then shed his disguise and opened a devastating and accurate fire. Badly hit by a hail of shellfire, and further damaged by a torpedo strike in the bow, HMAS *Sydney* limped away over the southern horizon, burning fiercely, and was never seen again. But the *Sydney*'s shots had found their mark too, starting fires that soon raged out of control. The German crew abandoned ship and succeeded in getting clear before *Kormoran*'s cargo of mines exploded, sending her to the bottom. Most of the German sailors were picked up by Allied ships off the Australian coast.

Scharnhorst *and* Gneisenau

Meanwhile, at the end of 1940, the Allied convoys had faced their most dire threat since the *Graf Spee* and the *Deutschland* had put

to sea more than a year earlier. On 28 December, the powerful battlecruisers *Scharnhorst* (Capt Hoffmann) and *Gneisenau* (Capt Fein), attempted to break out into the North Atlantic to attack merchant shipping. The attempt was thwarted when the *Gneisenau* was badly damaged in a storm off Norway on 2 January, causing the sortie to be abandoned, but three weeks later they again sailed from Kiel and, successfully eluding patrolling British cruisers, they replenished in the Arctic before breaking out into the Atlantic on the night of 3/4 February. On 8 February, in the North Atlantic, they sighted the British convoy HX106 east of Newfoundland, but the task force commander, Admiral Günther Lutjens, thought it prudent not to attack as the merchantmen were escorted by the battleship *Ramillies*. On 22 February, however, still about 925km (500nm) east of Newfoundland, they fell upon a westbound convoy which had dispersed and sank five ships totalling 25,784 tons.

On Saturday, 15 March 1941, the two warships were operating in the central North Atlantic when they encountered the scattered ships of another dispersed convoy. The result was a massacre. The *Gneisenau* sank seven freighters totalling 26,693 tons and captured three tankers of 20,139 tons, while the *Scharnhorst* sank six ships totalling 35,080 tons. *Gneisenau* had a narrow escape; as she was picking up survivors from her last victim, she was surprised by the battleship HMS *Rodney*, whose captain, alerted by a distress call, had detached his ship from convoy XH114 and rushed to the scene. Captain Fein, making good use of the *Gneisenau*'s superior speed and manoeuvrability, managed to avoid an engagement with his more heavily armed opponent, and got away.

Left: Admiral Förster, C-in-C German Fleet, takes leave of his officers on the bridge of the Admiral Scheer in Kiel. Förster was commander of the Gneisenau at the outbreak of World War II. Behind him is Captain Schniewind who succeeded him as C-in-C. At the time this photograph was taken, Schniewind was Chief of Staff to the Commander-in-Chief.

Top right: A close-up of the Gneisenau's forward 11in (280mm) guns. When the warship was decommissioned in July 1942, having been damaged in a bombing raid, her turrets were removed and used for coastal defence. Two were employed in Norway, and one at the Hook of Holland. It was intended to replace them with 15in (381mm) weapons during a refit, but the plan was abandoned in 1943.

Bottom right: The 'pocket battleship' Admiral Scheer seen before the war. When she was reclassified as a heavy cruiser she received a new raked bow; a new control tower and foremast replaced the original armoured tower, seen here.

Escape to fight another day

The British Admiralty immediately launched a major operation to trap the German warships, sending the battleships *Rodney* and *King George V* north, to join a third battleship, HMS *Nelson*, a cruiser and two destroyers in covering the Iceland passages. Meanwhile, Force H, with the battlecruiser *Renown*, the aircraft carrier *Ark Royal*, the cruiser *Sheffield* and some destroyers, set out from Gibraltar to cover the approaches to the French Atlantic ports, and on 20 March, a Swordfish reconnaissance aircraft from the carrier sighted the tankers captured by the *Gneisenau*. With

Force H coming up fast, the surprised crews were forced to scuttle two of the vessels, but the third managed to evade the British warships and reached the Gironde estuary. The two German battlecruisers were also sighted by a Swordfish later in the day, but the aircraft had radio trouble, and by the time its sighting report was transmitted, the warships had slipped away. On 22 March, they were met by the torpedo boats *Iltis* and *Jaguar* and some minesweepers and escorted into Brest. Their sortie had cost the Allies 22 ships totalling 115,622 tons. Fortunately for the Allies, the two ships were to remain penned up in the French Channel

ports, under almost continual air attack, until February 1942, when they made a dash through the English Channel to regain their North German harbours.

The careers of the 'Admirals'

Also menacing the Allied lifelines at this time were the German heavy cruisers *Admiral Scheer* and *Admiral Hipper*, the former Panzerschiff *Admiral Scheer* having been re-classed as a heavy cruiser early in 1940. After spending most of 1940 refitting at Gdynia, the *Admiral Scheer* sailed on her mercantile warfare mission on 23 October, under the command of Captain Krancke, passing undetected through the Denmark Strait on 1 November after a replenishment stop at Stavanger. On 5 November, after sinking a solitary freighter, she attacked Convoy HX84, homeward bound from Halifax with 37 merchantmen and escorted only by the Armed Merchant Cruiser *Jervis Bay*. The latter's captain, E.S.F. Fegen, at once ordered the convoy to scatter under cover of a smokescreen and engaged the *Admiral Scheer*. The *Jervis Bay* was sunk with the loss of 191 crew, but Fegen's action (which earned him a posthumous Victoria Cross) had bought vital time for the convoy, which lost five ships to the *Scheer*'s guns.

Above: The heavy cruiser **Admiral Hipper** *was one of the most successful of all German warships. While raiding in the North Atlantic she sank 12 ships, and subsequently operated as part of a battle group in Arctic waters. She was bombed and scuttled at Kiel in May 1945.*

The *Admiral Scheer* then headed for the South Atlantic and the Indian Ocean, where she enjoyed considerable success before returning to the South Atlantic on 3 March. On 26–27 March, she evaded a British warship screen, passed through the Denmark Strait, and after a stop in Grimstadfjord (Bergen), she arrived in Kiel on 1 April 1941. During her sortie, she had sunk 17 ships totalling 113,233 tons.

The heavy cruiser *Admiral Hipper* (Captain Meisel), which had made several unsuccessful sorties into the Arctic during the summer of 1940, broke out into the Atlantic early in December via the Denmark Strait. On 24 December, 1,297km (700nm) to the west of Cape Finisterre, on the northwest tip of Spain, she intercepted the British troop convoy WS5A, comprising 20 ships bound for the Mediterranean. The convoy was escorted by the cruisers *Berwick*, *Bonaventure* and *Dunedin* and accompanied by the carriers *Argus* and *Furious*, destined for Takoradi on the west coast of Africa with reinforcement aircraft for the Middle East. Captain Meisel decided to attack, and in the ensuing engagement, on 25 December, the *Hipper*'s gunners hit the *Berwick* twice and damaged two transports. Because of engine trouble, which might have left his ship at the mercy of the British warships, Meisel elected to break off the attack and head for Brest, sinking one small freighter as he withdrew.

The *Hipper* left Brest on 1 February 1941 for another Atlantic sortie. On the 11th she located a straggler from a dispersed convoy and sank her, and on the 12th she made contact with nine unescorted ships of Convoy SLS64, sinking seven of them totalling 32,806 tons, and severely damaging two more. She returned to Brest on 15 February. A month later she sailed for Kiel, arriving on 28 March after an undetected passage through the Denmark Strait. She remained in German waters until 19 March 1942, when she deployed to Norway.

The demise of the auxiliary raiders

There were no new deployments of German armed cruisers in 1941. The next did not begin until 13 March 1942; *Michel*, with Cdr von Ruckteschell in command, left Flushing en route for the

Below: The 11in (280mm) guns of the battlecruiser Scharnhorst *in action. In company with* Gneisenau, Scharnhorst *destroyed 22 Allied ships during her commerce-raiding foray into the Atlantic, including the armed merchant cruiser* Rawalpindi.

Pacific. In 505 days at sea she sank or captured 18 ships totalling 127,107 tons. She spent two months in the spring of 1943 undergoing a refit at Kobe, Japan, Captain Gumprich assuming command in the meantime; August–September of that year found her operating in mid-Pacific. On 7 October, she began the return voyage to Japan, and 10 days later she was sunk by three torpedoes from the US submarine *Tarpon* 167km (90nm) east of Yokohama. One hundred and sixteen of her crew survived.

The next commerce raider, the *Stier* (Commodore Gerlach) took a more dangerous route to her operational area. Sailing from Rotterdam in May, she made a daring dash through the English Channel under strong escort and succeeded in reaching the Atlantic, where during the next four months she sank four ships totalling 29,406 tons. In her last action, on 27 September 1942, she was severely damaged by return fire from the sinking American freighter *Stephen Hopkins* (Captain Paul Buck) and had to be abandoned, her crew being picked up by the blockade-runner *Tannenfels*.

The last attempt by the Germans to deploy a commerce raider took place on 10 February 1943, when the *Coronel* (Captain Thienemann) also attempted to break out into the Atlantic through the Channel. Damaged in an attack by Westland Whirlwind fighter-bombers, she sought refuge in Boulogne and, after surviving further air attacks, she returned to Kiel via Dunkirk, and later served as a fighter direction ship in the Baltic. After the war she became a Norwegian Auxiliary vessel under the name of *Svalbard*.

FAST ATTACK: THE S-BOATS

The Germans called them *Schnellboote* – fast boats; the British name for them was E-boats. They presented an enormous threat to Britain's coastal convoys, and their audacious crews achieved some spectacular successes.

On the night of 27/28 April 1944, nine S-boats – fast attack craft – of the 5th and 9th Flotillas slipped out of Cherbourg harbour, their assigned mission being to intercept a British convoy that coastal radar stations had reported off Selsey Bill, to the east of the Isle of Wight. As the flotilla commanders brought their craft across the broad mouth of Lyme Bay, intent on attacking the convoy from the south-west, they were amazed to see eight US American tank landing ships (LSTs), escorted by a single British corvette. The Germans had no means of knowing it, but

Above: S-boats moored alongside a depot ship. The German MTBs were between 80 and 100 tons in displacement, had crews of up to 25 men and, with their three diesel engines, could reach speeds of between 36 and 40 knots.

Left: A German S-boat at speed. After the fall of France, the S-boat flotillas redeployed from their bases in northern Germany to Dunkirk and Boulogne, in order to attack British coastal traffic in the Straits of Dover.

Above: *One of Germany's first S-boats, S2, was originally built for Yugoslavia as the* Velebit. *Taken over by Italy in 1941, she was renumbered MAS 2. Seized by Germany after Italy's surrender, she was again renumbered S2.*

Below: *S-boats on operations in the Atlantic at about the time of the Allied invasion of Normandy. Air attack was a constant danger, and anti-aircraft armament was progressively increased. Great vigilance was required when moving at high speed.*

Above: S12 *approaching its depot ship. This S-boat was one of a batch of four built in 1934 at the Lürssen shipyard, Vegesack. They displaced 78 tons and had a 21-man crew. Original armament was a single 20mm AA gun and two torpedo tubes.*

they had stumbled on a dress rehearsal for the forthcoming Allied invasion of Europe. The LSTs, putting out from the harbours of Plymouth and Brixham, were heading for Slapton Sands in South Devon, where the troops on board and their armoured fighting vehicles were to simulate the actual American D-Day landing on

Utah Beach. As well as the corvette *Azalea*, the convoy should also have been escorted by the destroyer HMS *Saladin*, but she had been damaged in a collision with a landing craft in Plymouth harbour, and no replacement had been assigned.

The S-boats quickly closed in for a torpedo attack, and in an engagement lasting only a few minutes, they sank two LSTs and badly damaged another. Five destroyers were summoned to the scene, and pursued the German boats across the Channel, but the speedy enemy craft got clean away. American casualties were heavy; according to official figures, 441 soldiers and 197 seamen perished, but even today there is controversy over the actual loss of life, some sources putting it as high as 749. The action of Slapton Sands was the biggest triumph of the *Kriegsmarine*'s coastal forces in World War II, and it was kept a secret by the Allied nations for a long time afterwards.

The German Navy's *Schnellboote* – S-boats – were in action from the very beginning of World War II, the 1st Flotilla operating in the Baltic as part of the naval forces covering the German invasion of Poland. Built mainly by the Lürssen shipyard at Vegesack and Schlichting of Travemünde, they came in various sizes, being up to 35m (115ft) long and displacing up to 105 tons. Their three-shaft diesel engines gave them a maximum speed of anything up to 78km/h (42 knots); they had a combat radius of 1,297km (700nm) at 55km/h (30 knots), and were generally armed with two 20mm AA guns, which could also be used for surface actions, and two 53cm (21in) torpedo tubes. In place of spare torpedoes, the larger types could carry up to eight mines.

The *Schnellboote* were known to the Allies as E-boats, a name bestowed upon them by the British early in the war to signify 'enemy boat'. Their first encounter with the Royal Navy occurred on the night of 9/10 May 1940, during the Norwegian campaign, when four craft of the 2nd S-boat Flotilla from Wilhelmshaven attacked the cruiser *Birmingham* and seven destroyers making a sortie against German minelayers in the Skagerrak. Although one boat, the *S31*, hit the destroyer HMS *Kelly* with one torpedo amidships, she remained afloat and was towed to Newcastle-on-Tyne for repair.

S-boats at Dunkirk

At the end of May 1940, the 2nd S-boat Flotilla presented a serious threat to the shipping engaged in evacuating the British Expeditionary Force from France. Six boats, operating in relays of three, were to enter the northern part of the English Channel under cover of darkness and attack any British vessels British vessels sighted, preferably those homeward bound with their cargoes of troops.

Left: *Operational service on an S-boat was rigorous. Their bridges were armour-plated from 1943 to give some protection from the cannon fire of low-flying Allied fighters. Some 250 of these fast attack craft were built in total.*

Top right: *The speedy S-boats could have created havoc among the ships evacuating the British Expeditionary Force from Dunkirk, had they been available in sufficient numbers. Here, hundreds of troops rush over to the starboard side of a French destroyer as it capsizes. It is almost certainly the Sirocco, which was sunk by torpedoes from S23 and S26 on 31 May.*

Bottom right: *An S-boat at speed in the English Channel. The larger S-boats were capable of carrying six or eight mines instead of spare torpedoes, and minelaying became an important part of their activities throughout the war.*

Above: A G7 torpedo is hoisted on board an S-boat. At the beginning of World War II, the Germans had two basic torpedo warheads, the G7a and the G7e, inside an almost identical casing. The 'G' stood for the diameter of 533mm (21in), the '7' for the length of 7m (22.9ft).

Below: Two S-boat flotilla commanders: Lieutenant Commanders Klaus Feldt (left) and Niels Bätge. On 12 December 1942, the latter's 4th S-boat flotilla attacked a British convoy off Lowestoft and sank five freighters.

Right: The tiny cramped engine room that was the S-boat's nerve centre. The diesel engines of the later S-boats produced 7500hp and could generate a speed of up to 42 knots. Maximum combat radius was in the order of 700 miles at 30 knots.

The first three craft, *S25*, *S30*, and *S34*, entered the Channel area without incident on 28 May, *S34* (Lieutenant Obermaier) sinking a small steamer soon after taking up station. Some time later, Lieutenant Zimmermann in *S30* sighted a vessel with the aid of his night glasses and identified it as a British destroyer. Starting *S30*'s engines, he closed to action stations and began his attack. At 0045 on 29 May, he launched four torpedoes at the target, which was the destroyer HMS *Wakeful*. Hit by at least one torpedo, the destroyer, laden with troops lifted from the beaches of Dunkirk, was torn in half, and sank with heavy loss of life.

On 31 May, the French destroyer *Sirocco* was sunk by the *S23* (Lieutenant Christiansen) and *S26* (Lieutenant Fimmen), and on the next day Lieutenant Obermaier in *S34* sank the armed trawlers *Argyllshire* and *Stella Dorado*.

With the British Expeditionary Force – and also many French troops who had fought their way back to the coast – withdrawn to England, the S-boats, now able to operate from Dutch, Belgian and French harbours, turned their attention to mercantile traffic

Above: Lt Cmdr Klaus Feldt, commander of the 2nd S-boat Flotilla, receiving the Knight's Cross from Captain Bütow, Commander S-boats. Bütow was later promoted rear-admiral, and given command of the 10th Escort Division in the Baltic.

Below: S-boats moored alongside their depot ship Tsingtau in Swinemünde harbour. The Tsingtau and another depot ship, the Carl Peters, *supported groups of S-boats escorting freighters during the German invasion of Norway in April 1940.*

in the English Channel, sinking a tanker, a freighter and a coaster in June.

Early British countermeasures

To counter the S-boat threat, the British Admiralty established a flotilla of five motor torpedo boats (MTBs) at Dover, but as yet they were greatly outnumbered. In any case, the S-boats were faster, bigger and better armed than the British craft, and it required skill and judgement, which would only come with operational experience, to get the better of them.

S-boat operations in the English Channel were stepped up in July 1940, when the *Kriegsmarine* and *Luftwaffe* joined forces in attacks on British coastal convoys as a prelude to the planned invasion of Britain. Air attacks would be followed up by S-boat sorties against stragglers and damaged vessels, the surface attacks normally being carried out by craft of Lieutenant Commander Birnbacher's 1st S-boat Flotilla, operating from newly established bases in Holland. In one operation of this kind, against a coastal convoy passing through the Straits of Dover on 8 August 1940, 11 out of 21 ships, mostly colliers, were sunk or damaged. In another attack by the 1st S-boat Flotilla, this time on a convoy off Great Yarmouth on 4 September, four S-boats sank six freighters totalling 9,996 ton).

By the winter of 1940–41, attacks by S-boats, whose numbers had now been reinforced, presented an increasingly serious threat to British coastal convoys, and in December 1940, as a countermeasure, the 6th Motor Gunboat (MGB) Flotilla was formed. It consisted of three previously converted boats, armed with four

Above: S14, seen here before the outbreak of World War II, was one of a batch of four craft completed in 1934 at Vegesack. She did not serve operationally in World War II, being used as a training boat in the Baltic.

Lewis guns and one Oerlikon, and five boats originally built for the French Navy; these were armed with four Lewis guns and four .303 Browning machine guns in a Boulton Paul power-operated turret. In March 1941, the 6th MGB Flotilla deployed to Felixstowe and was soon in action against the enemy, joining the existing MTB flotillas in patrolling lines from the Humber to the Hook of Holland, and from Texel to the Thames. The Coastal Forces, as these light craft flotillas were collectively known, were to be greatly expanded before the end of 1941.

Successes in the Channel

Early in 1941, the S-boats added minelaying to their activities, creating more problems for the Admiralty, as mines were accounting for more ships sunk and damaged than any other weapon. By this time another S-boat flotilla, the 3rd, was operational under the command of Lieutenant Commander Kemnade, and on the night of 7/8 March, 12 S-boats from 1st and 3rd Flotillas made a sortie against a British convoy and sank seven freighters. This exploit was followed, on 18 March, by a bold foray by six boats of the 1st Flotilla into the Humber Estuary, when one freighter was sunk.

The 3rd S-boat Flotilla's stay in the Channel area was short-lived. In April 1941, it redeployed to the Baltic in readiness for the forthcoming German invasion of Russia, being replaced by the

2nd Flotilla under Lieutenant Feldt. The latter was quickly in action, sinking two freighters and damaging a third in an attack on a convoy off Great Yarmouth on 17 April. Activity by the S-boats gradually tailed away as the long summer nights approached, and in July and August, the 2nd and 1st Flotillas both redeployed to the Baltic, the former to assume a minelaying mission on the approaches to the Soviet naval bases in the north. The 2nd Flotilla would return in October, but in the meantime responsibility for S-boat operations in the North Sea and Channel areas rested with a new unit, the 4th Flotilla, which began attacking convoys in August. Before the end of the year the 6th Flotilla, commanded by the highly experienced Lieutenant Obermaier, was also operational.

On 12 February 1942, the 2nd, 4th and 6th S-boat Flotillas, combined to provide part of the escort for the *Scharnhorst*, *Gneisenau* and *Prinz Eugen* during the warships' dash through the English Channel, the S-boats covering the Dutch coastal area. After this operation, the S-boat flotillas were increasingly occupied with escort duty and minelaying, protecting the seaward flanks of German coastal convoys, or providing protection for blockade run-ners, now becoming increasingly vital to Germany's war effort, as they approached their home ports.

A shift onto the defensive

In the autumn of 1942, the 5th S-boat Flotilla deployed to the Channel area under Lieutenant Commander Klug and, with the other three flotillas, was soon in action against British coastal convoys, the Germans taking advantage of the fact that many of the Royal Navy's escort vessels had been temporarily transferred to duty in the Atlantic; here they strengthened the escort groups guarding the troop convoys destined for the invasion of North Africa. The period of renewed success against the British merchant traffic lasted only as long as the escort destroyers were absent, and early in 1943, with RAF Coastal Command's newly formed anti-shipping strike wings becoming more effective, S-boats moved

Below: *The S-boats often worked in conjunction with the* **Möwe**-*class torpedo boats, seen here escorting the* **Scharnhorst, Gneisenau** *and* **Prinz Eugen** *during the famous 'Channel Dash' of 12 February 1942.*

increasingly over to the defensive, lending their firepower to German coastal convoys.

The S-boat flotillas, however, were still capable of powerful offensive action. On 27 February 1943, for example, four boats of the 5th S-boat Flotilla carried out a particularly daring attack, penetrating into Lyme Bay and attacking a convoy that had assembled there. In a matter of minutes, they torpedoed and sank the freighter Moldavia (4,858 tons), a tank landing craft and two escort vessels, both armed trawlers.

On several occasions in the spring of 1943, attempted attacks on British convoys were frustrated by the prompt action of destroyer escorts and also by air attacks, delivered mostly by Spitfires and Hawker Typhoon fighter-bombers. The Dutch coast was a favourite hunting ground, being within easy range of the RAF fighter squadrons based in East Anglia. However, on the night of 13/14 April, Lieutenant Commander Klug's 5th S-boat Flotilla carried out another audacious raid when four boats attacked a heavily escorted convoy off the Lizard Head, Cornwall, and hit the destroyer *Eskdale* with two torpedoes, stopping her dead in the water. She was sunk a few minutes later by two other S-boats,

Left: The helmsman of an S-boat at his post. Note the traditional wheel. Most S-boats were built at the Lürssen yard, Vegesack, although some were produced by Schlichting of Travemünde and Werf Gusto, Schiedam.

Below: Torpedoes in storage at a base on the Atlantic coast of France, August 1944. The Kriegsmarine experienced constant problems with its torpedoes, which often failed to detonate or exploded prematurely, and therefore harmlessly.

Above: *In March 1942, the S-boat S111, pictured here, was one of several craft carrying out a mining operation off the southeast coast of England when they were attacked by British MTBs. S111 was badly damaged, and sank under tow.*

Right: *A Bristol Beaufighter Mk X, showing its underwing rocket projectile rails. Beaufighters and Mosquitoes equipped the strike wings of RAF Coastal Command from 1943, and carried out anti-shipping attacks along the coasts of German-occupied Europe.*

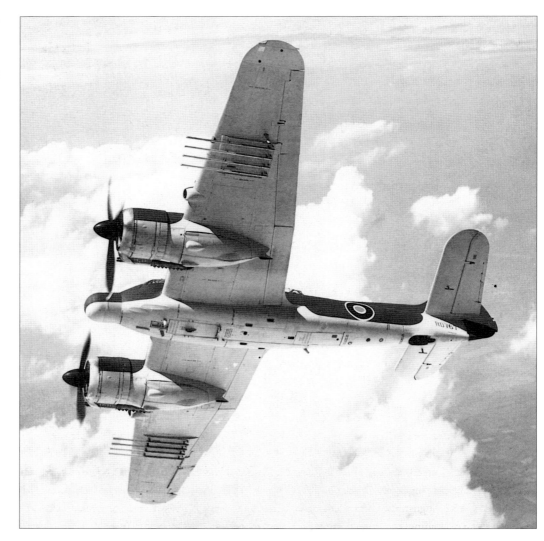

Above: Young German engine room artificers at their battle station. Maintaining the three diesel engines, which were often overworked by high-speed combat runs, was a heavy burden of responsibility.

which also accounted for the 1,742-ton freighter *Stanlake*. All four S-boats returned to their base without loss.

In the summer of 1943, with the long hours of daylight again curtailing S-boat raids into British coastal waters, all the flotillas based on the Channel coast were engaged in minelaying activities. The S-boats made 77 sorties during this period, laying a total of 321 mines, mostly off the Isle of Wight and Lyme Bay.

The S-boats were very difficult to attack in harbour, as they were ensconced in special concrete pens. It was when they were in transit between ports, creeping along the coast, that they were at their most vulnerable. Three boats were lost in transit and several more damaged in July and August 1943, the victims of British MTBs and Typhoons. On 11 August, the latter successfully broke up a convoy of seven S-boats, sailing into the French port of L'Abervach in

readiness for a sortie against shipping in Plymouth Sound.

In the spring of 1944, with the build-up to the Allied invasion of Europe well under way, the S-boat flotillas had a profusion of targets among the shipping that crowded Britain's south coast harbours, and the Slapton Sands debacle proved that, given the opportunity, the S-boats could still wreak enormous havoc. One of the units involved in this spectacular attack, the 9th Flotilla under Commodore von Mirbach, had only recently been deployed to the Channel area. In general the 9th Flotilla operated in concert with the 5th, now under the command of Lieutenant Commander Karl Müller, a highly capable officer much respected by his British counterparts and known to them as 'Charlie'. The word that 'Charlie was out' on a particular night was certain to provoke a considerable response from the British coastal forces. In one spectacular attack on a convoy off south-west England on the night of 5/6 January 1944, seven S-boats of the 5th Flotilla swamped the escort with salvoes of torpedoes, forcing the British warships to make violent evasive manoeuvres, and broke through to sink three freighters and a naval trawler.

Right: The RAF's 12,000lb (5443kg) bomb was the first completely streamlined heavy bomb to be used during World War II, and was the forerunner of the 22,000lb (9979kg) Grand Slam. The 'Tallboy' combined great penetrative power – it was designed specifically to penetrate through many feet of concrete – with tremendous blast effect. It was used with great effect against German weapons installations on the continent, including the S-boat pens at Le Havre. Only the Avro Lancaster was powerful enough to carry it.

Some of the most intense actions during this period were fought in the North Sea, where S-boats were carrying out minelaying operations off Grimsby and Great Yarmouth. In the English Channel, a combination of radar and rapid reaction by the escort forces were gradually getting the better of the S-boats by the spring of 1944; nevertheless, there were some heated engagements. The majority of the attacks were beaten off by the convoy escorts, now greatly strengthened by the addition of light cruisers.

S-boats at Normandy

As was the case with Germany's U-boats, the presence of strong Allied naval forces guarding the flanks of the invasion prevented the S-boat flotillas from interfering with the armada of ships transporting the troops to their Normandy beaches on 6 June 1944. However, in the days that followed, the S-boats made repeated attempts to attack the steady stream of resupply vessels in the Channel. In the first two nights after the first wave of the invasion, they sank three tank landing ships (LSTs) and a number of smaller craft, but they lost four of their own number to enemy action; on 14 June, the 2nd Flotilla, making for Le Havre in daylight, was attacked by two squadrons of RAF Beaufighters, which sank three more. Before nightfall, the RAF turned its heavy bombers loose, sending 221 Lancasters to attack the main S-boat base at Le Havre. They attacked in two waves, dropping 1230 tons of bombs,

including several of the new 5436kg (12,000lb) Tallboys, which caused much devastation among the S-boat pens. Thirteen craft were destroyed and the commander of the 5th Flotilla, now Lieutenant Commander Johanssen, was killed. Despite their losses, the S-boat commanders continued to make night sorties into the Normandy assault area throughout June, their numbers dwindling and torpedo stocks running low after 5 July, when 41 torpedoes were destroyed in an explosion at the Le Havre repair depot. By mid-July, most of the surviving S-boats were concentrated on Boulogne.

In August 1944, the offensive capability of the S-boat flotillas received a boost when they began to receive the new long-range T3D *Dackel* (Dachshund) torpedoes. The new weaponry brought about a change of tactics; the boats now operated in groups of six, three launching the *Dackels* and the other three acting as torpedo-carriers. Results, however, were disappointing. In a series of sorties against shipping in the Seine Bay during the first two weeks of August, 77 *Dackels* were expended and only one freighter sunk, although other vessels were damaged, including the cruiser HMS *Frobisher*.

With the Allies consolidating their hold on Normandy and advancing inland, the *Kriegsmarine* was forced to concentrate its S-boat operations in the northern part of the English Channel and the North Sea, deploying the 8th Flotilla (Commodore Zymalows-

Above: *A Lancaster preparing for a night take-off. Most of the 'Tallboy' precision attacks were carried out by aircraft of No. 617 Squadron, the famous 'Dambusters' squadron which, in May 1943, destroyed the Mohne and Eder dams in the Ruhr.*

Below: *An aerial view of Le Havre, taken some time in October 1944, showing clouds of dense black smoke rising from the oil tanks, and grey smoke rising from the dock warehouses after an attack by RAF Bomber Command.*

ki) to Boulogne from Rotterdam. From this base, the flotilla made sporadic and unsuccessful attacks against British shipping, but on the night of 3/4 September, the last 13 operational S-boats in the Channel area moved to Rotterdam and Ijmuiden, one boat being sunk en route by the Dover batteries. By the end of the year some 40 S-boats were still operating from Dutch bases against convoys sailing between the Thames and the River Scheldt, as well as against east coast and Channel convoys. Mines laid by the S-boats still constituted a severe threat; between January and May 1945, mines laid by the S-boats alone sank 31 merchantmen totalling 89,000 tons.

Deployment to the Mediterranean

In March 1945, the British Second Army crossed the Rhine south of the Dutch frontier, and swung north to cut off all land access to the German forces in Holland, which meant that the S-boats were now entirely dependent on supplies arriving by sea. Despite this, and despite rising losses, they went on fighting to the last. Early in April, five S-boats were sunk in quick succession during mining operations in the Humber Estuary and on the Thames-Scheldt route, and on the night of 13/14 April, during a minelaying operation by 12 boats of the 4th, 6th and 9th Flotillas, they fought their last action against British warships off the Scheldt estuary. In the last days of the war in northwest Europe, an operation was tentatively

Above: An S-boat picks up speed in the Atlantic on 26 May 1942. S-boat crews had to be ever at the ready to make a quick pursuit of enemy craft.

planned in which the surviving S-boats were to have transported *Linsen* (Lens) one-man explosive boats to within striking distance of the Allied shipping which crammed the Scheldt estuary. It would almost certainly have been a suicide mission; fortunately for the crews, it came to nothing.

S-boats arrived in the Mediterranean during the closing weeks of 1941, when the 3rd Flotilla was transferred from the Baltic to Derna, Libya, under the command of Lieutenant Commander Kemnade. S-boats operated only sporadically in the Baltic thereafter until the end of 1944, when the 5th Flotilla was redeployed from the Channel area to assist in the evacuation of German personnel from the Baltic states. The 3rd Flotilla carried out its first operation in the Mediterranean, a mining sortie to Malta, in December, and minelaying remained its principal activity until June 1942, when it began offensive operations against the Malta supply convoys. In its first action, it sank the destroyer HMS *Hasty* and damaged the cruiser HMS *Newcastle*. Early in 1943, after more minelaying operations, it operated against Allied convoys off Algeria. Following the Allied conquest of North Africa, it moved to the naval base at Taranto, where it remained until 8 September 1943, two days before the Italians surrendered.

Now, only two boats remained, *S54* and *S61*. As they left Taranto harbour, their crews dropped some mines, one of which sank the fast minelayer HMS *Abdiel* on 10 September with heavy loss of life. As they passed through the Adriatic en route for Venice, the two boats caused more havoc, sinking an Italian destroyer and a gunboat – legitimate targets now that Italy had surrendered – and capturing the new Italian troop transport *Leopardi* with 700 troops on board. Reaching Venice with their fuel tanks almost dry, they compelled the local commander to surrender and took over the city until reinforcements arrived.

The second S-boat Flotilla to deploy to the Mediterranean, in the summer of 1943, was the 7th, under Commodore Trummer. Operating from southern France, it reached its operational area just in time to see action against the Allied naval forces supporting the landings on Sicily. On the night of 16/17 July, in an engagement with British MTBs, five of its boats were severely damaged, effectively putting it out of action as a cohesive unit until repairs could be effected. In fact, it was mostly inactive until December, when seven of its boats laid mines off the west coast of Italy. There is no record of any further major operations.

Baltic and Black Sea Operations

The 1st S-boat Flotilla, meanwhile, had been deployed to the Baltic in June 1942 as part of the naval force supporting the attack, by the German 11th Army, on the fortress of Sevastopol. During the battle for the Taman Peninsula, in September, its boats sank 19 Russian freighters evacuating troops to Novorossisk. In subsequent operations against Soviet shipping on the Caucasus coast, its boats enjoyed considerable success, in most cases operating in concert with Italian MTBs, and having frequent engagements with Soviet patrol cutters and torpedo cutters. As time went by, the S-boat crews were subjected to increasing air attacks as the Soviet Air Force grew in effective strength, and began to put pressure on the German forces as the latter went on to the defensive. In October 1943, the 1st Flotilla joined with the Italian 3rd Motor Minesweeper Flotilla in defending the Kerch Straits against attacks by Soviet warships, as the German evacuation of the Kuban bridgehead was in progress.

In April 1944, the 1st S-boat Flotilla formed part of the naval force covering the evacuation of German and Romanian forces from the Crimea to Constanza; after that, there is no further record of its operations. In all, 249 S-boats served with the Kriegsmarine during World War II, including a number of foreign boats, mostly Italian, that were either captured or taken over. Of this total, 157 were lost or scuttled. Of the surviving 92, 30 went to the USA, 34 to Britain, and 28 to the USSR at the war's end.

Below: This photograph of an S-boat travelling at speed in the English Channel shows the armament to good advantage. One 40mm gun is positioned at the stern, while a quickfiring 20mm is located forward.

CAPITAL SHIPS

At the outbreak of World War II, Germany's capital ships were among the most powerful in the world. Few in number though they were, it took all the Royal Navy's resources to track them down to their eventual destruction.

At dawn on 1 September, 1939, the old pre-dreadnought battleship *Schleswig-Holstein*, one of the few capital ships that Germany had been permitted to retain under the terms of the Armistice, fired the opening shots of World War II against the Polish fortress of Westerplatte. Joined later in the month by her sister ship, the *Schlesien*, she continued to batter Polish fortifications on the Hela Peninsula until they too were overwhelmed. At the close of the Polish campaign, the two old battleships returned

Above: The 'pocket battleship' Admiral Scheer *at her launch at Wilhelmshaven, 30 June 1934. The* Scheer *and her two sisters, the* Deutschland *and the* Graf Spee, *represented attempts to build a capital ship within the limitations of the Versailles Treaty.*

Left: The battleship Schleswig-Holstein *was one of three pre-dreadnoughts retained in the post-World War I German fleet, the others being* Hannover *and* Schlesien. *All were rearmed.*

to training duties in the Baltic until April 1940, when the *Schleswig-Holstein* led a battle group covering transport vessels that were landing troops in Norway. The *Schlesien* was held in reserve, ready to lend supporting fire as necessary.

Back once more with the *Kriegsmarine* Fleet Training Squadron in the Baltic, the two vintage battleships continued to fulfil their cadet training role until the night of 18/19 December 1944, when Avro Lancasters of RAF Bomber Command dropped 824 tons of bombs on the port of Gdynia, sinking the *Schleswig-Holstein* and several other vessels. The *Schlesien* was once more assigned to bombardment duty in March and April 1945, shelling Soviet forces advancing along the shores of the Gulf of Danzig. On 2 May 1945, only days before Germany's unconditional surrender, she was badly damaged by a mine at Swinemünde, her hulk being beached and blown up by the retreating Germans. Ironically, the *Schleswig-Holstein* and *Schlesien* both outlasted the two ultra-modern battleships that were designed to replace them, the *Bismarck* and *Tirpitz*.

The pride of the new German fleet

The first of them, the *Bismarck*, was laid down on 1 July 1936 at the Hannover shipyard of Blohm und Voss, and was launched on 14 February 1939 by Dorothea von Löwenfeld, grand-daughter of Prince Otto Eduard Leopold von Bismarck-Schönhausen, the Prussian statesman and chancellor of the First Reich, for whom the battleship was named. Completed in August 1940, the *Bismarck* began sea trials in the Baltic soon afterwards. Up to that time, the world had never seen a warship like her. From stem to stern she measured 248m (813ft); the armour plating on her turrets and sides, made of specially hardened Wotan steel, was 33cm (13in)

Below: *The battleship* Schlesien *was launched in May 1906 and served with the High Seas Fleet in World War I, taking part in the Battle of Jutland. In 1917 she was used as a drill ship and accommodation vessel, and ended the war as a cadet training ship. She was reconstructed between the wars.*

Above: *The battleship* Schleswig-Holstein *bombarding Polish positions at Westerplatte on 1 September 1939. These were the opening shots of the war that was to engulf the world for six years. The* Schleswig-Holstein *survived the conflict, although damaged by bombing in 1944, and was scuttled in 1945.*

Left: *'Painting ship' was a chore detested by the sailors of all navies the world over. Here, seamen touch up the waterline of the* Schleswig-Holstein. *Like her sister ship* Schlesien, *the old battleship was reconstructed between 1931 and 1935, bridging the gap until the completion of more modern capital ships.*

thick. Listed as 35,000 tons to comply with the London Treaty, she was in fact 42,000 tons standard displacement and over 50,000 tons fully laden. With her main armament of eight 38cm (15in) guns and a speed of 54km/h (29 knots), she could outpace and outfight anything else afloat. The officer appointed to be her commander was Captain Ernst Lindemann, a 45-year-old Rhinelander. For most of his 2000-strong crew, *Bismarck* was their first ship; their average age was 21.

Because of delays resulting from unexpected technical problems, *Bismarck*'s sea trials were not completed until the spring of

Above: Loading heavy shells on to a capital ship. German naval gunnery was excellent in both world wars, thanks to very good rangefinding equipment. The heavy armament of German capital ships usually comprised 11in (280mm) or 15in (380m) guns.

Above: Ernst Lindemann, captain of the battleship Bismarck; *at that time he was 45 years old. As a naval cadet Lindemann graduated top of his term. Clever and cool, he was a chain-smoker and drank huge amounts of coffee.*

1941. Based on Gdynia, she now embarked on a series of exercises and was joined by the new 14,000-ton heavy cruiser *Prinz Eugen*, commanded by Captain Helmuth Brinkmann. On 2 April 1941, the German Naval Staff issued orders for *Bismarck*'s operational deployment. Together with *Prinz Eugen*, she was to break out into the Atlantic via the Denmark Strait, and join up with the battlecruiser *Gneisenau*, which had arrived at Brest a fortnight earlier after its commerce-raiding foray. The *Scharnhorst* was also to have joined them, but essential repairs were being made to her boilers. Yet even without the *Scharnhorst*, the German battle group possessed formidable power, and the British Admiralty, whose grip on the Denmark Strait passage was slender, was well aware of the carnage that would ensue if the warships made concerted attacks on the Atlantic convoys.

Unexpected setbacks for the battlefleet

Then, on 6 April, there occurred the first in a series of events that was to disrupt the German battle plan completely. At dawn that day, a Bristol Beaufort torpedo-bomber of RAF Coastal Command penetrated Brest harbour and flew through intense flak to strike *Gneisenau* on the waterline with one torpedo, putting the battlecruiser out of action for months. The aircraft was shot down with the loss of all four crew; its pilot, Flying Officer Kenneth Campbell, was posthumously awarded the Victoria Cross.

The *Gneisenau* was further damaged by RAF Bomber Command on the night of 10/11 April 1941, when she was hit by four bombs. Bomb damage to the harbour facilities also delayed the repairs to the *Scharnhorst*. Then, on 24 April, the *Prinz Eugen* was damaged by a magnetic mine, and it would take a fortnight to make repairs.

All these misfortunes left the German Navy C-in-C, Admiral Raeder, with only two options. Either he could postpone the sortie until *Bismarck*'s sister ship, the *Tirpitz*, was ready to join her; or he could order *Bismarck* and *Prinz Eugen* to sail at the earliest opportunity. Conscious of the facts that the approach of summer would soon strip away the cover of darkness from the Arctic route, and that *Tirpitz* was only just about to begin her trials, he chose the latter option.

On 18 May 1941, with the task force commander, Admiral Günther Lütjens, aboard the *Bismarck*, the two warships carried out a final exercise in the Baltic and then sailed westwards independently. On 20 May, the force was reported in the Kattegat by the Swedish cruiser *Gotland*, and intelligence of the enemy force's northward movement reached the British Admiralty early the next day. As soon as he received intelligence that they had passed through the Kattegat, Admiral Sir John Tovey, the C-in-C Home Fleet, increased surveillance of the northern passages into the Atlantic, ordering the battleship *Prince of Wales*, the battlecruiser *Hood* and six destroyers to sail from Scapa Flow under Vice-Admiral L.E. Holland, flying his flag in the *Hood*, while reconnaissance aircraft were dispatched to search for the enemy warships. Throughout the night of 21 May, the latter steamed northwards up the Norwegian coast, following a zigzag pattern to avoid British submarines.

At 0900 on 22 May, *Bismarck* entered Korsfjord and then Grimstad fjord, just south of Bergen, while *Prinz Eugen* went into

Right: Captain Helmuth Brinkmann of the heavy cruiser Prinz Eugen. *A classmate of Lindemann's, Brinkmann was later promoted to Vice-Admiral and commanded escort forces in the Black Sea, supporting convoys attempting to relieve the besieged fortress of Sevastopol.*

Below: The gunnery training ship Bremse *also had a minelaying role. She was sunk off North Cape in September 1941, by the British cruisers* Nigeria *and* Aurora.

Kalvanes Bay, to the north-west. Lütjens signalled the cruiser to take on oil from one of the tankers that had been deployed to support the warships and to be ready to sail in the evening.

Had Lütjens elected to sail directly to the Arctic, and made rendezvous with the tanker that was waiting there, he might yet have eluded the trap the British were setting for him. As it was, the two warships were photographed in their fjords by a Photographic Reconnaissance Unit Spitfire, and a second sortie, by a Royal Navy Martin Maryland, revealed that the vessels had departed.

The hunt for the Bismarck

Admiral Tovey now deployed the main body of the Home Fleet to Icelandic waters to reinforce the heavy cruisers *Norfolk* and *Suffolk*, which were patrolling the Denmark Strait. Three more cruisers were guarding Lütjens' alternative breakout route, between Iceland and the Faeroes. At 1922 on 23 May, the *Bismarck* was sighted by the *Suffolk*, emerging from a snow squall in the Denmark Strait, and the British cruiser began to shadow her. About an hour

Above: The battleship **Bismarck** *pictured during completion. Centre foreground, with his back to the camera, is Adolf Hitler, on a visit to the vessel. Hitler was fascinated by battleships, and memorized vast amounts of technical information about them, but knew nothing about sea power and its applications, leaving all decisions to Admiral Raeder.*

Top right: The battleship **Bismarck***, the most powerful warship afloat in 1941. She and her sister,* **Tirpitz***, were the largest German battleships actually built with a large percentage of weight devoted to armour protection. The original design had a straight stem, which was altered to a clipper bow, as seen here.*

Bottom right: The battlecruisers **Scharnhorst** *and* **Gneisenau** *snapped by a British photo-reconnaissance aircraft in dry dock at Brest after their sortie into the Atlantic. The two warships are at lower centre, partially obscured by smoke from generators placed close by. Attempts to bomb them cost the RAF dearly.*

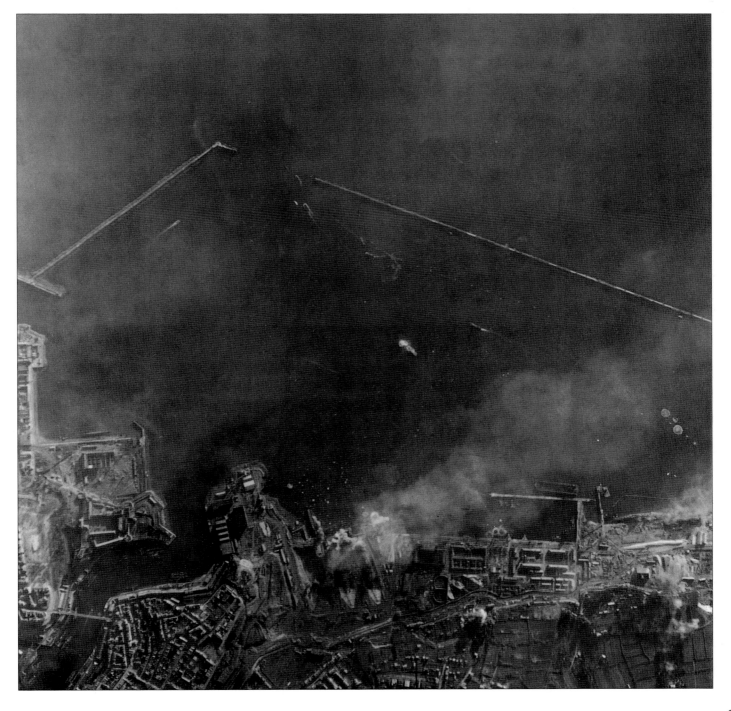

Above: Seen from the heavy cruiser Prinz Eugen, *the battleship* Bismarck *fires a salvo from her 15in (381mm) guns. This photograph was taken in the Baltic during sea trials, a few weeks before* Bismarck's *ill-fated voyage.*

Right: Admiral Sir John Tovey, commander of the British Home Fleet, who masterminded the hunt for the Bismarck. *Although mainly remembered for this action, his warships were also responsible for the safe passage of Britain's vital Atlantic convoys.*

later, the *Suffolk* was joined by the *Norfolk*, which came under enemy fire at a range of 11,880m (13,000 yards) and was straddled by three 38cm (15in) salvoes before retiring under cover of smoke, miraculously undamaged. She radioed her enemy-sighting report to Admiral Tovey, whose main fleet was still some 1110km (600nm) to the south-west. The two cruisers continued to shadow Lütjens' ships at high speed throughout the night, the *Suffolk* maintaining radar contact with the enemy.

Bismarck *sinks the* Hood

Meanwhile, the new battleship *Prince of Wales* and the battlecruiser *Hood*, dispatched ahead of the main British force, were coming up quickly. Vice-Admiral Lancelot Holland, commanding these two powerful units from the *Hood*, was anticipating a night

*Above: The battlecruiser HMS **Hood**, seen at Portsmouth in 1937, after returning from a patrol off the Spanish coast during the civil war. Much admired by the British public, she was the mightiest warship in the world up to World War II, and was one of the most keenly felt losses of the entire war.*

action; his plan was to concentrate the fire of his heavy ships on the *Bismarck*, leaving the cruisers to deal with the *Prinz Eugen*. He was unaware that the *Bismarck* was no longer in the lead; the blast from her guns during her brief action with the *Norfolk* had put her forward radar out of action, so Lütjens had ordered the *Prinz Eugen* to change position.

As his heavy ships approached, Admiral Holland, conscious of the need for surprise, imposed strict radio and radar silence, relying on the *Suffolk*'s reports to keep him informed of the enemy's

position. The cruiser lost contact for nearly three hours during the night, but when she regained it at 0247 Holland turned his ships on to an interception course, increasing speed to 52km/h (28 knots). At 0537, the opposing forces sighted each other at a range of 31km (17nm), and opened fire at 0553. Both German ships concentrated their fire on the *Hood* and, thanks to their stereoscopic rangefinders, hit her almost immediately. At 0600 she was hit again by a salvo which pierced her lightly-armoured decks and detonated in her after magazines. She blew up with a tremendous explosion, broke in two and sank with alarming speed. Only three of her crew of 1,419 officers and ratings survived.

The *Prince of Wales* now came under heavy fire, sustaining hits by four 38cm (15in) and three 20cm (8in) shells, one of which exploded on the bridge and killed or wounded almost everyone there except her captain, J.C. Leach, who ordered the battleship to

Above: The Bismarck *at anchor. With her powerful armament and good all-round protection, the* Bismarck *was more than a match for any single Allied warship.*

turn away under cover of smoke. The *Prince of Wales* was so newly completed that she had not yet finished working-up; the contractors were still working on her 35.5cm (14in) turrets when she sailed, and she was therefore not fully battleworthy. This, and the fact that his ship had sustained serious damage, persuaded Leach that his only valid course of action was to assist the cruisers in maintaining contact with the enemy until Admiral Tovey's main force could reach the scene.

The *Bismarck*, however, had also suffered, taking three hits from *Prince of Wales*'s heavy armament. Two of her fuel bunkers were now leaking oil, and others were contaminated. Lütjens was now forced to make a weighty decision: to abandon the commerce-raiding sortie and steer south-west for St Nazaire, the only port on the Atlantic coast of France with a dry dock large enough to accommodate his flagship while repairs were carried out.

Closing in for the kill

The main body of the Home Fleet was still 612km (330nm) to the south-east and could not expect to make contact until 0700 on 25 May at the earliest. However, other ships were also heading for the scene. The Gibraltar-based Force H was now heading north to intercept the German squadron, and the battleships *Rodney*, *Revenge* and *Ramillies* and the cruiser *Edinburgh* were also released from escort duties to take part in the chase. The main concern now was to

Above: The destruction of the Hood, *as depicted by a Time-Life artist. Of her 1419 crew, only three were saved.* Hood *was the flagship of Vice-Admiral Lancelot Holland, who was among the dead. The battleship* Prince of Wales *is in the foreground.*

reduce the *Bismarck*'s speed, giving the hunters a chance to close in for the kill, and at 1440 on 24 May Admiral Tovey ordered the carrier *Victorious* to race ahead to a flying-off point 185km (100nm) from the enemy ships and launch a Swordfish strike against them.

The Swordfish crews, in appalling weather conditions, found the *Bismarck* alone; Lütjens had already detached the *Prinz Eugen* to make her own way to the French Channel ports, which she reached without incident. *Bismarck* was hit by one torpedo out of the nine launched at her without suffering significant damage. At 0300 on 25 May, Lütjens altered course to the south-east, and at this critical juncture the shadowing cruisers, which had been following at extreme radar range, lost contact. This, and the fact that the bulk of the Home Fleet went off on a wild goose chase after receiving some erroneous bearings transmitted by the Admiralty, caused considerable delay in the pursuit before the British realized Lütjens was probably heading for the Biscay ports. Luckily the Admiralty had already instructed Force H to position itself on a line from which its ships and aircraft could intercept the *Bismarck*, should she follow this course of action.

'We fight to the last shell'

On the morning of 26 May, *Bismarck* was sighted nearly 1,297km (700nm) west of Brest by a Catalina maritime reconnaissance aircraft and by two Swordfish from the carrier *Ark Royal*. A Swordfish strike was laid on, and almost ended in disaster when some of the 14 aircraft sent out attacked the cruiser *Sheffield* – detached from Force H to make radar contact with the *Bismarck* – in error. Fortunately, thanks to a combination of effective evasive manoeuvring by the cruiser and faulty magnetic pistols fitted to the torpedoes, no damage was caused.

At 1910, *Ark Royal* launched a second strike of 15 Swordfish, which succeeded in hitting the German battleship with two torpedoes. One struck the *Bismarck*'s armoured belt and did little damage, but the other struck her extreme stern, damaging her

propellers and jamming her rudders fifteen degrees to port. At 2140 Admiral Lütjens signalled Berlin: 'Ship no longer manoeuvrable. We fight to the last shell. Long live the Führer.'

A boost to Allied morale

The doomed *Bismarck* was shadowed by five British destroyers throughout the night, and determined but unsuccessful torpedo attacks were made upon her. Soon after daybreak, the battleships *King George V* and *Rodney* came within range and opened fire from 14,600m (16,000 yards). By 1020 the *Bismarck* had been reduced to a blazing wreck, with all her armament out of action, but she was still afloat despite the fact that the two British battleships had fired over 700 shells at her. The gunnery action continued until the British battleships had to withdraw for replenishment, leaving the cruisers *Norfolk* and *Dorsetshire* to close in and finish off the *Bismarck* with torpedoes. She sank at 1036, her colours still flying, in position 48⁻10'N, 16⁻12'W, some 480km (300 miles) west of Brest, taking all but 119 of her crew of over 2,000 officers and men with her. The destruction of the *Bismarck* brought massive relief to the British Government. 'Had she escaped,' Winston

Above: Fairey Swordfish torpedo-bombers of the Fleet Air Arm. It was an attack by Swordfish from the aircraft carrier HMS **Ark Royal** *that sealed the* **Bismarck**'s *eventual fate. A torpedo hit on her stern jammed her steering mechanism.*

Right: The battlecruiser **Scharnhorst**, *followed by the* **Gneisenau**, *steams at speed through the English Channel during the famous 'dash' of 12 February 1942. The photograph is taken from the* **Prinz Eugen**, *the third heavy warship involved.*

Churchill wrote later, 'the moral effects of her continuing existence as much as the material damage she might have inflicted on our shipping would have been calamitous. Many misgivings would have arisen regarding our capacity to control the oceans, and these would have been trumpeted around the world to our great detriment and discomfort.'

Meanwhile, Captain Brinkmann's plan to take the *Prinz Eugen* on a lone commerce-raiding sortie into the South Atlantic had been thwarted by continual engine trouble, leaving him no alternative but to make for Brest. She evaded the British air and sea

Above: The Commander (Battleships) of the **Kriegsmarine,** *Vice-Admiral Ciliax, inspecting the crew of the* **Scharnhorst,** *accompanied by Captain Hoffmann (right) and executive officers. Together the* **Scharnhorst, Gneisenau,** *and* **Prinz Eugen** *made a formidable battle unit.*

patrols – although she was sighted once by a Coastal Command aircraft – and reached her destination on 1 June. She remained in the Biscay ports for the rest of the year, together with the *Scharnhorst* and *Gneisenau*, under persistent attack by the RAF while the Royal Navy hunted down the commerce raiders' supply ships one by one. In June 1941, five tankers and three supply ships, plus a number of weather observation vessels, were destroyed or scuttled after being intercepted.

The deployment of the **Tirpitz**

The *Bismarck* was gone; but the threat of her powerful sister ship, *Tirpitz*, was still on the horizon. Launched in April 1935, *Tirpitz* had been completed only a few weeks before *Bismarck* met her

end, and spent most of 1941 undergoing her sea trials, after which she was designated flagship of the Baltic Fleet. In November 1941, however, it was decided that she should deploy to Norwegian bases for offensive action against the Arctic convoys to Russia, with a secondary defensive role against a possible British landing in northern Norway. On the night of 16/17 January 1942, she accordingly sailed for Trondheim under the command of Captain Topp.

Above: The battlecruiser Gneisenau *at sea. The term 'battlecruiser' was a British appellation; the Germans always referred to the* Scharnhorst *and* Gneisenau *as battleships.* Gneisenau *was decommissioned in July 1942 having been damaged in an RAF raid on Kiel.*

Right: Admiral Otto Ciliax, *architect of the 'Channel Dash', later conducted operations against Allied convoys in Arctic waters. His flagship was the* Tirpitz, *the last of Germany's modern battleships.*

Her deployment, however, was part of a much greater scheme of things. The *Kriegsmarine* was growing short of fuel oil, making it difficult to sustain long-range raiding operations in the Atlantic. Shorter-range missions against the Allied convoys in Arctic waters were a different prospect, and so the plan now was to assemble a powerful battle group, with *Tirpitz* as its nucleus, for operations in this new theatre of war.

The 'Channel Dash'

On 12 February 1942, as part of this overall scheme, the *Scharnhorst, Gneisenau,* and *Prinz Eugen* slipped out of Brest harbour and embarked on their famous dash through the English Channel, intent on gaining the north German ports as a preliminary step before re-deployment to Norway. All did not go according to plan. Although the three warships succeeded in beating off

Above: This splendidly clear photograph of the Tirpitz *in Narvikfjord was taken by a PRU Spitfire in July 1942. The protective anti-torpedo nets are clearly visible. They did not prevent the battleship being badly damaged by midget submarines.*

Top left: Fleet Air Arm aircrew are briefed for a strike on the Tirpitz *in Altenfjord, Norway, on 3 April 1944. The battleship was hit by 14 bombs, with 122 dead and 316 wounded. Four British aircraft were lost in the attack.*

Bottom left: The heavy cruiser Prinz Eugen *sighted by air reconnaissance in Hjelte Fjord, Norway. After service in Northern waters,* Prinz Eugen *was transferred to the Baltic, where her heavy guns were used to support the German army.*

British air and surface attacks, the *Scharnhorst* and *Gneisenau* both struck mines en route. On 13 February the *Scharnhorst* limped to safety in Wilhelmshaven while the other two warships went on to the Elbe Estuary. A fortnight later, *Gneisenau* was hit by Bomber Command in Kiel harbour and never went to sea again; her gun turrets were removed for coastal defence, and she was sunk as a blockship at Gdynia, where she was seized by the Russians and broken up between 1947 and 1951. Only the *Scharnhorst*, as we shall see later, would re-emerge in due course to threaten Allied shipping on the high seas.

On 6 March, the *Tirpitz*, flying the flag of Vice-Admiral Ciliax and accompanied by three destroyers, set out to intercept convoys PQ12 and QP8, the first bound for Murmansk, the second on its way home. The convoys passed each other off Bear Island

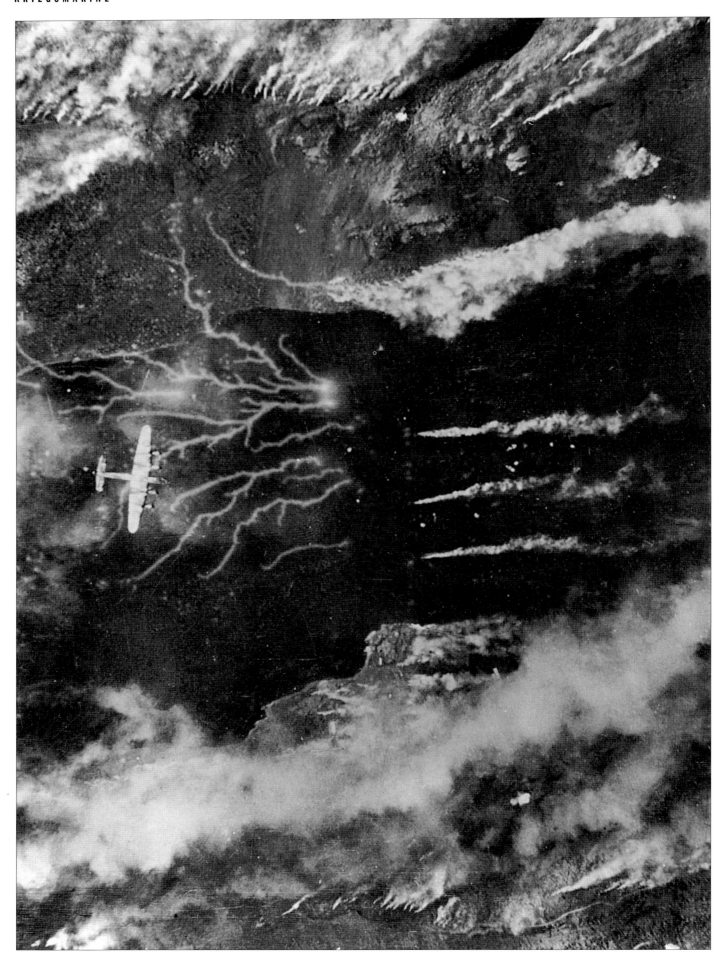

the next day, but the German force made no contact, and Ciliax ordered it to withdraw southwards. Strong units of the British Home Fleet, aware of the German force's movements thanks to intercepted radio signals, sailed on an interception course. At daybreak on the 9th, a reconnaissance Albacore from the carrier *Victorious* spotted the *Tirpitz*, which was then subjected to a torpedo attack by 12 Fairey Albacores. The attack, unfortunately, was car-

ried out in line astern, which gave the *Tirpitz* ample room to avoid all the torpedoes, although one did pass within 9.1m (30ft) of her. Two Albacores were shot down. The failure of this attack was a bitter disappointment for the Royal Navy, but it did have one significant result; on Hitler's orders, the *Tirpitz* was never to put to sea again if carrier-based aircraft were known to be in the vicinity.

Left: *On 15 September 1944, the* Tirpitz *was further damaged by six-ton 'Tallboy' bomb dropped by one of 27 Lancasters that attacked her from a base in north Russia. After this attack, the battleship was used as a semi-static artillery battery.*

Below: *The Fleet Air Arm's bombs bursting on and around the* Tirpitz *during the attack of 3 April 1944. This raid (Operation Tungsten) clearly demonstrated the efficacy of the divebomber – in this case, the Fairey Barracuda – against stationary vessels.*

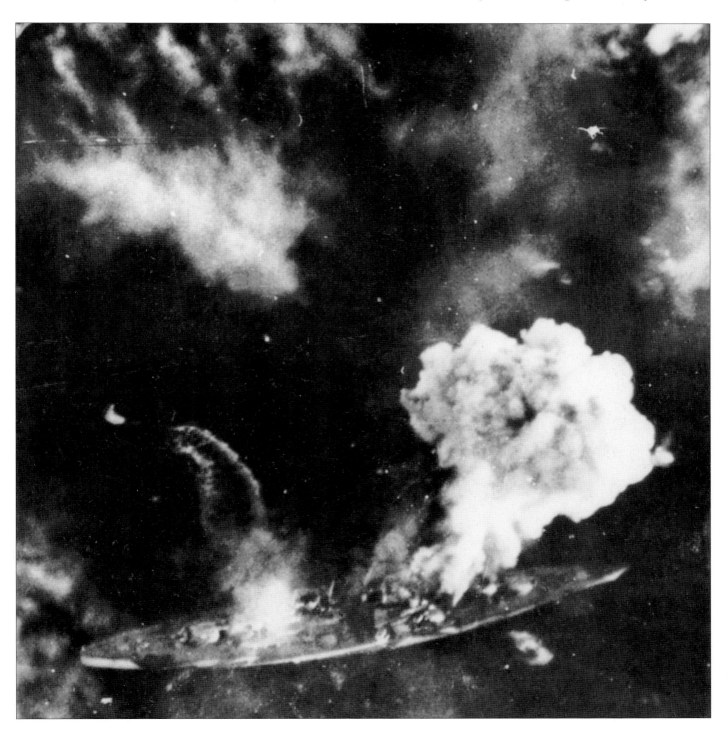

On 11 March, the battleship entered Narvik, and the following day she returned to Trondheim, where over the next few weeks she survived a number of attacks by Halifax bombers of the RAF. By this time, the German naval force in Norway had been strengthened by the arrival of the *Admiral Hipper*, *Admiral Scheer* and *Lützow*, presenting a truly formidable threat to the Allied convoys.

Tirpitz: *a latent threat*

Tirpitz's next sortie did not take place until the summer, against the Russian-bound Convoy PQ17, which sailed from Iceland in June with 36 freighters and a strong naval escort. As soon as it learned of PQ17's departure, the Naval High Command initiated Operation Rösselsprung (Knight's Move), its aim the total destruction of the convoy. On the afternoon of 2 July, Force I under Admiral Schniewind, comprising the battleship *Tirpitz* and the cruiser *Admiral Hipper* with four destroyers and two torpedo boats, set out from Trondheim, and the next day Vice-Admiral Kummetz's Force II, comprising the heavy cruisers *Lützow* and *Admiral Scheer*, with five destroyers, sailed from Narvik and headed north to join Force I at Altafjord, where they waited for more information on the strength of the convoy's escort. On 5 July, *Tirpitz* sortied from Altafjord but made no contact with the convoy; a Soviet submarine, the *K21* (Captain 2nd Class Lunin) fired a salvo of torpedoes at her, which missed.

In the event, the fate of Convoy PQ17, which was ordered to scatter in the belief that *Tirpitz* and other warships were about to attack, was sealed by U-boats and aircraft, which sank 24 ships between them. This disaster, and the continued presence of the *Tirpitz* and other heavy units in northern Norway, persuaded the Allies to suspend convoys to Russia during the Arctic summer, when the cover of darkness was stripped away.

A reminder that the battleship was still active came on 8 September 1943, when she emerged to bombard the island of Spitzbergen. Two weeks later, however, she was damaged in Altaford by a daring midget submarine attack, and two further attacks by Fleet Air Arm dive-bombers in the summer of 1944 rendered her unseaworthy. Nevertheless, it was not until she was capsized and sunk by RAF Bomber Command, whose Lancasters dropped 5435kg (12,000lb) bombs on her while she was at anchor

Right: Allied personnel examine one of Tirpitz's *massive propeller shafts. The process of cutting up the battleship went on for several years; some 900 crew members and civilian workers were entombed in the hull.*

Below: The capsized hulk of the Tirpitz *lies in Tromsofjord after the attack by Lancasters, November 1944. The two squadrons involved, No.s 9 and 617, each claimed to have sunk the ship, beginning a friendly rivalry that lasts to this day.*

off Tromso, that the British Admiralty could finally relax. A considerable amount of planning, manpower and flying hours had gone into the destruction of a ship which, in the event, had inflicted very little damage on Allied shipping.

Scharnhorst *is lured to its doom*

By that time, the other principal surface threat to Allied shipping, the *Scharnhorst*, had also been removed. She had arrived in Norway in March 1943, joining the other heavy units at Altafjord, and in September she had accompanied *Tirpitz* in the bombardment of installations on Spitzbergen. She did not put to sea again until December, and this time it was to engage the Arctic convoys. After an interval of several months, when no convoys had passed to Russia because of the dangers involved, they had resumed in November when Convoy RA54A sailed from Archangel to the UK without incident; two more outward bound convoys, JW54A and JW54B, also made the journey from Loch Ewe to Russia unmolested. The next two convoys, however, were both reported by the *Luftwaffe*, and Admiral Dönitz issued orders that they were to be attacked, not only by the 24 U-boats based

Above: Survivors of the Scharnhorst *stand about under guard on the catapult deck of the* Duke of York. *They are wearing merchant seamen's rescue kit.*

on Bergen and Trondheim, but by available surface units, the largest of which was the *Scharnhorst*.

The convoys were JW55B, outward bound from Loch Ewe with 19 ships, and RA55A, homeward bound from Kola. The former sailed on 20 December 1943, the latter three days later. Each was escorted by ten destroyers and a number of smaller vessels.

At 1400 on Christmas Day, the *Scharnhorst* – now under the command of Captain F. Hintze and flying the flag of Admiral Bey, a former commodore of destroyers who had recently been appointed to command the Northern Battle Group – sailed from Norway accompanied by five destroyers to intercept JW55B, which had been located by air reconnaissance on 22 December. The convoy had already been attacked by Ju 88s and by U-boats, but without success. On 26 December, Admiral Bey ordered his destroyers to form a patrol line to search for the convoy in heavy seas. He knew that a British cruiser covering force comprising the

Belfast, Norfolk and *Sheffield* was operating in the Barents Sea; what he did not know was that there was also a distant covering force commanded by the C-in-C Home Fleet, Admiral Sir Bruce Fraser, and comprising the battleship *Duke of York*, the cruiser *Jamaica* and four destroyers, which had sailed from Iceland.

Fraser, aware that JW55B had been located by enemy aircraft, was convinced that the *Scharnhorst* would make a sortie against it, and detached four destroyers from Convoy RA55A, which he did not consider to be under immediate threat, to reinforce JW55B's close escort. His hope was that this strengthened destroyer force would not only be sufficient to drive off the *Scharnhorst*, but might perhaps damage her enough for the *Duke of York* to come up and finish her off. At this point, Fraser's ships were 370km (200nm) SW of North Cape and the cruiser force, under Admiral Burnett, 278km (150nm) to the east.

Admiral Bey's five destroyers, meanwhile, had not only failed to locate the convoy; they had also, because of a signalling error, lost

Below: Blindfolded for security reasons, the Scharnhorst survivors are taken ashore at a British port on their way to a prisoner-of-war camp. The Germans later recorded that their rescuers treated them with great kindness.

touch with the flagship and were subsequently ordered to return to base, so that they took no part in the coming events. At 0840 on the 26th, the cruisers *Norfolk* and *Belfast* obtained radar contact with the *Scharnhorst* at 32,000m (35,000 yards), and at 0921 the *Sheffield* glimpsed her in the stormy darkness at 11,895m (13,000 yards). A few minutes later, all three destroyers opened fire on the battlecruiser and obtained three hits, one of which put her port 15cm (6in) fire control system out of action. The *Scharnhorst* replied with a few harmless 28cm (11in) salvoes, then Bey turned away to the south-east while Burnett placed his cruisers between the threat and the convoy, screened by four destroyers from the escort.

At 1221, the three cruisers again sighted the *Scharnhorst* and opened fire with full broadsides at 10,065m (11,000 yards), while the destroyers fanned out to attack with torpedoes. Before they were able to get into position, the battlecruiser retired to the north-east, her gunfire having put one of *Norfolk*'s turrets and all her radar out of action; *Sheffield* also suffered some splinter damage. But the *Scharnhorst* had taken punishment too, including a hit abreast 'A' turret and one on her quarterdeck.

At 1617 the *Duke of York*, now 37km (20nm) away to the north north-east, obtained a radar echo from the *Scharnhorst*, and at 1650 Fraser ordered *Belfast* to illuminate her with starshell; immediately

afterwards, the *Duke of York* opened fire with her 35.5cm (14in) armament. Admiral Bey was now trapped between Burnett's cruisers to the north and Fraser's warships to the south, and he had no choice but to fight it out. Once *Scharnhorst*'s gunners had recovered from their surprise their fire was accurate, but although they straddled the British battleship many times, they failed to register a serious hit on her. The *Duke of York*'s gunnery was excellent; she scored 31 straddles out of 52 broadsides, with enough hits to put the battlecruiser's 'A' and 'B' turrets out of action and to rupture some steam pipes, which reduced her speed so that Bey had no chance of outrunning his adversaries, even if the opportunity had arisen.

At 1824 the third of *Scharnhorst*'s turrets was put out of action, and Fraser, realising that the *Duke of York*'s 35.5cm (14in) shells,

fired at short range with a flat trajectory, were unlikely to pierce the enemy's armour, turned away to let the destroyers finish the job. Two of them, the *Savage* and *Saumarez*, approached from the north-west under heavy fire, firing starshell, while *Scorpion* and *Stord* attacked from the south-east, launching their torpedoes at 1849. As Hintze turned his ship to port to engage them, one of *Scorpion*'s torpedoes struck home, closely followed by three more from the first two destroyers. As the small ships retired under cover of smoke, the *Duke of York* and the cruisers closed in to batter the enemy warship with merciless fire.

By 1930, the battlecruiser was a blazing wreck, her hull glowing red-hot in the Arctic night, and the destroyers closed in to finish her off with torpedoes. At 1945 she blew up; only 36 of her crew of

Above: *Admiral Wilhelm Meendsen-Bohlken, the last commander of the German surface fleet (with head lowered), is informed by Commander R. J. Richards, RN, that he is under arrest. The German admiral has just been ordered off his yacht, the* Hela.

Left: *The 'pocket battleship'* Lützow *(formerly* Deutschland*) was badly damaged on several occasions in the course of the war, but survived almost to the very end, being sunk by RAF 'Tallboy' bombs in shallow water in Swinemünde in April 1945.*

Right: *Admiral Otto Schniewind commanded the powerful German naval force which might have dealt devastating blows to the Allied Arctic convoys.*

1,968 officers and men were rescued from the freezing seas. So ended the Battle of North Cape, and with it the last attempt by a German capital ship to challenge the supremacy of the Royal Navy. All the other major surface units that had served with the Northern Battle Squadron – the *Lützow*, *Admiral Hipper* and *Admiral Scheer* – had now been transferred to the Baltic, together with the *Prinz Eugen*, where all except the latter would be destroyed or damaged beyond repair by air attack in the last days of the war.

CRUISERS AND DESTROYERS

The campaign in Norway decimated Germany's light cruisers and destroyers, but her heavy cruisers remained a force to be reckoned with. Operating in concert with powerful new destroyers, they menaced the vital Arctic convoys.

The German invasion of Norway in April 1940, successful though it was, cost the *Kriegsmarine* dearly in ships sunk and lives lost. The heavy cruiser *Blücher* was an early casualty; on the first day of the invasion, 9 April, she was bound for Oslo with 2000 troops on board when she was sunk by torpedoes and gunfire in the Drobak Narrows – the entrance to Oslofjord – with the loss of over 1000 officers and men.

The *Admiral Hipper*, last of the five original German heavy cruisers launched before World War II, made her first war sortie on 18 February 1940, when she accompanied the *Scharnhorst* and

Above: The heavy cruiser Blücher, *ablaze and capsized after being hit by shellfire and torpedoes in Oslofjord during the German invasion of Norway, on 9 April 1940. She had enjoyed only a short career, having been launched in 1937.*

Left: The destroyer Georg Thiele *(Z2), second of the 16 ships that comprised the* Leberecht Maass *class. Ten of this class were sunk in World War II.* Georg Thiele *was scuttled after sustaining heavy damage at the Second Battle of Narvik, on 13 April 1940.*

Above: *The* Blücher, *seen here, was one of five heavy cruisers in the* Kriegsmarine, *the others being the* Seydlitz, Prinz Eugen, Lützow, *and* Admiral Hipper. Lützow *was sold to the Soviet Union in 1940 and was later bombed in Leningrad.*

Below: *The* Admiral Hipper *was by far the most successful of Germany's heavy cruisers. On one occasion during her commerce-raiding activities, she sank seven out of nine ships in the Atlantic on 12 February 1941. She was bombed and scuttled in May 1945.*

Above: The light cruiser Karlsruhe *was the first of her class to be launched, on 20 August 1927. She made several cruises as a training ship prior to World War II. Badly damaged by a British submarine, she was sunk by German surface forces in April 1940.*

Gneisenau on Operation Nordmark, the search for Allied convoys between Britain and Scandinavia. During the invasion of Norway, she was the flagship of Task Group 2, whose objective was Trondheim. On 8 April, as she headed for her objective, she was engaged by the destroyer HMS *Glowworm*, which rammed her just before sinking. On 10 April, the damaged *Admiral Hipper* left Trondheim and headed south for Germany, accompanied by a destroyer. She was at sea again in June, taking part in the sortie in which the *Scharnhorst* and *Gneisenau* sank the aircraft carrier *Glorious*. Later in the year, as we have already seen, she broke out into the Atlantic on a commerce raiding expedition.

Of the six light cruisers available at the outbreak of World War II, two were sunk during the Norwegian campaign. During the invasion, the *Karlsruhe* (Captain Rieve) was the flagship of Task Group 4, heading for Kristiansand; on 9 April she was torpedoed by the British submarine *Truant*, and was so badly damaged that she had to be sunk later by a German torpedo boat, while on the

Left: Two crewmen of the light cruiser Karlsruhe. *The wearing of uniform was obligatory at all times, even on shore leave. Each man carried a* Soldbuch *(Pay Book) which included a passport-type photograph and personal details.*

Right: After the war Nürnberg, *having surrendered to the Allies in Copenhagen, was incorporated into the Soviet Navy as the* Admiral Makarov. *Based at Kronstadt, she was used as a training ship until 1956, and was broken up in 1959.*

Below: Launched in December 1934, the light cruiser Nürnberg *took part in the Non-Intervention Patrol during the Spanish Civil War. Her World War II career mostly involved mining operations and training.*

following day the *Königsberg*, part of the Bergen-bound Task Group 3, fell victim to an air attack by 16 Blackburn Skua dive-bombers of the Fleet Air Arm, flying from Hatston in the Orkney Islands. The bombing was highly accurate and the cruiser, having suffered three direct hits and a dozen near misses, exploded and sank. She was the first major warship to be sunk by air attack in war. The wreck of the *Königsberg* was refloated in 1943 and dry-docked, but was abandoned and broken up after it capsized in September 1944.

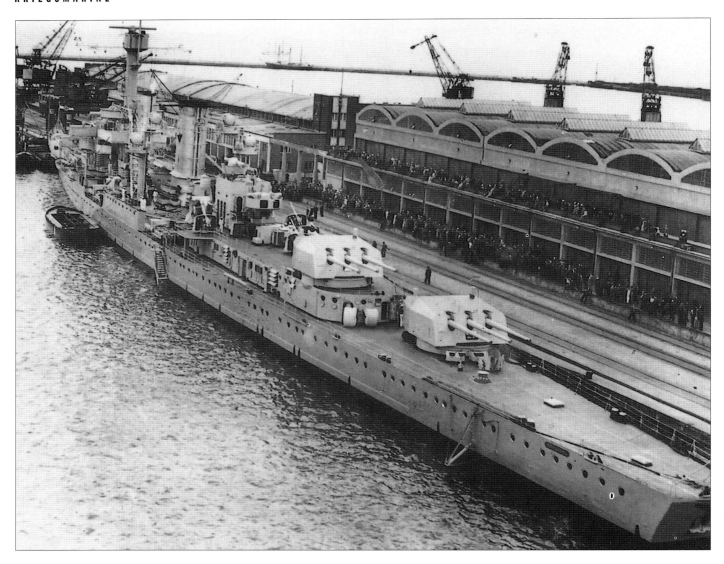

Below: The Königsberg *in action. Light cruisers of this class carried a main armament of eight 5.9in (150mm) guns and a secondary anti-aircraft armament. They had a combat radius of 5300 miles (8527km) at 18 knots.*

Above: The light cruiser Königsberg, *seen here at Wilhelmshaven, was flagship of the Senior Officer, Scouting forces, in the early part of World War II. She was sunk at Bergen by Skua dive-bombers of the Fleet Air Arm on 10 April 1940.*

Nürnberg: *an unremarkable career*

In September 1939, the light cruiser *Nürnberg* was the flagship of Vice-Admiral Densch, commanding the German Naval Reconnaissance Forces, and from 3 September, with other light cruisers, she was active in laying mines in the North Sea. On 12 December 1939, she was attacked by the submarine *Salmon* and received a torpedo hit in the bow. After repair she returned to active duty in the summer of 1940, first in Norwegian waters, and then with the Fleet Training Squadron in the Baltic. In September 1941, she participated in the blockade of the Soviet Baltic Fleet. She saw

Right: The light cruiser Köln *was built at the Wilhelmshaven Naval Yard and launched on 23 May 1938. After service in northern waters, she operated against Soviet naval forces in the Baltic. She was bombed and sunk at Wilhelmshaven on 30 April 1945.*

little action until 13 January 1945, when she carried out defensive mining operations in the Skagerrak, fighting off several attacks by British aircraft. On 9 May she surrendered to the Allies at Copenhagen, alongside the *Prinz Eugen*, and in January 1946, she was turned over to the Russians at Libau, subsequently serving in the Soviet Navy as the *Admiral Makarov*.

The light cruisers *Leipzig* and *Köln* also carried out mining operations in the North Sea area during the early weeks of the war, prior to participating in the invasion of Norway. Both were subsequently transferred to the Baltic (the *Köln* after serving in Norway during 1942–3), where they took part in operations against Soviet forces. On 15 October 1944, the *Leipzig* was badly damaged in a collision with the *Prinz Eugen* off Gdynia. The *Köln* was bombed and sunk at Wilhelmshaven on 30 April 1945, while the *Leipzig* – having taken part in the evacuation from East Prussia, despite her unseaworthy condition – surrendered to the Allies and was sunk in the North Sea in July 1946, laden with canisters of poison gas.

Top left: The heavy cruiser Admiral Hipper *fitting out at Wilhelmshaven in 1939. The* Hipper *spent most of her operational career in northern waters, then served with the Fleet Training Squadron in the Baltic. Surviving considerable damage at the Battle of the Barents Sea in 1942, she was scuttled on 3 May 1945.*

Bottom left: Provisions, including fresh meat, are taken on board a light cruiser. Considerable priority was given to maintaining high-quality food standards on German warships, even at times of acute shortages during World War II.

Below: The light cruiser Leipzig *carried out a number of mining operations in the North Sea before being damaged by a torpedo from HM submarine* Salmon *in December 1939. She was later assigned to the Fleet Training Squadron in the Baltic.*

Early destroyer operations

At the outbreak of World War II, the *Kriegsmarine* was armed with two classes of destroyer; the *Diether von Roeder* class, comprising six ships, and the *Leberecht Maass* class of sixteen. The two classes were very similar in size and displacement, although the *von*

Right: A Heinkel He 60 float-plane flies over the light cruiser Köln. *The He 60 served on all the major German warships until replaced by the more modern He 114 and Arado Ar 196. It continued to serve in various capacities well into World War II.*

Below: The Leberecht Maass, *first of the 1934-type destroyers, seen at her commissioning ceremony in 1937. She was an early casualty of the war, being mined and sunk in the North Sea off Borkum, on 22 February 1940.*

Above: The Admiralty yacht Grille *(Cricket) was the first ship in the Kriegsmarine to test the high-pressure steam machinery that was designed for use in the new class of German destroyer.* Grille *was laid down in 1934 and commissioned in May 1935.*

Right: Grille *was used as a minelayer until February 1942. She was subsequently decommissioned and used as a staff ship at Narvik for the C-in-C and Commander (Submarines) Arctic. She was sold to private owners in the US and broken up in 1951.*

Roeder class, the last of the pre-war destroyers, had a superior performance, being capable of 70km/h (38 knots) against the *Leberecht Maass*'s 30. Range was better, too; 4,850nm at 35km/h (19 knots) against 4,400nm at the same speed. Both classes carried an armament of five 12.7cm (5in) guns, four or six 37mm AA guns, eight or 12 20mm AA guns, eight 53cm (21in) torpedo tubes, and 60 mines. Each class carried a complement of 315. All German destroyers in the North Sea area were under the operational command of Vice-Admiral Densch's Reconnaissance Forces, and in the early months of the war were mainly engaged in minelaying, an activity that resulted in many shipping loses. The losses, however, were not all one-sided; on 22 February 1940, the German destroyers *Leberecht Maass* and *Max Schultz* were mined and sunk in the North Sea, northwest of Borkum, and for the Germans there was worse to come.

Heavy casualties at Narvik

Early in the morning of 10 April 1940, in poor visibility, five ships of the British 2nd Destroyer Flotilla entered Ofotfjord and attacked a force of German destroyers which had been landing troops. They sank the *Wilhelm Heidkamp* (killing the Officer Commanding Destroyers, Commander Bonte) and the *Anton Schmitt*, and also damaged the *Diether von Roeder* and *Hans Lüdemann*. Two British destroyers, the *Hardy* and *Hunter*, were sunk by other German destroyers as they withdrew, and the British commander, Captain B.A. Warburton-Lee, was killed. The British ships also sank several merchantmen and a German supply ship, the *Rauenfels*.

On 13 April, the Admiralty sent nine destroyers, covered by the battleship *Warspite*, to comb the fjords for the eight surviving German vessels, which were starved of fuel because their supply tanker had not arrived. All eight were destroyed by gunfire and torpedoes in the action that became known as the Second Battle of Narvik, or were scuttled by their crews. It would take some time before these losses could be recouped.

Top right: The destroyer **Hans Lüdemann** *was the first of the* **von Roeder** *class to be launched, in 1938. Five of the six boats, including* **Lüdemann,** *were sunk during the Norwegian campaign, dealing a damaging blow to the* **Kriegsmarine***'s light forces. More than a year would pass before any new-build destroyers would enter service.*

Bottom right: The wrecks of German destroyers scattered around Narvik Fjord. The warships of the Narvik force, having disembarked troops, were taken completely by surprise. The force commander, Commander Bonte, was among those who lost their lives.*

Below: The **Diether von Roeder** *(Z17) was leader of a class of six destroyers, all of which were commissioned just before the outbreak of World War II. Damaged by Royal Navy destroyers at the Second Battle of Narvik, she was scuttled on 13 April 1940.*

Top left: A German troop transport off the coast of Norway, April 1940. The vessel on the left of the photograph is a T1-type torpedo boat. Destroyers played an essential role in protecting the invading forces.

Bottom left: German troops disembark at Narvik on 9 April 1940. The operation was carefully planned and well executed, but the German forces – particularly the Kriegsmarine – suffered substantial casualties. Air power was the key to success.

Above: Unloading small-arms ammunition from a German warship in 1940. The handlers are German naval personnel; the crossed flags above the chevron on the sleeve of the man on the right indicate that his trade is Signalmeister (Signaller).

A depleted force

This early British success meant that, by the middle of April 1940, therefore, the German destroyer force had been reduced to 10 ships out of the original 21. Twelve more ships, designated Z23–Z34, had already been laid down, but the first would not be ready for service until early in 1941; in the meantime, the much reduced destroyer force was occupied mainly with minelaying activities, or with escorting other minelaying craft in the North Sea and English Channel areas.

On 17 October 1940, Bey led the destroyers *Hans Lody, Karl Galster, Friedrich Ihn,* and *Erich Steinbrink* in a sortie towards the western exit of the Bristol Channel; there was a confused engagement with British cruisers and destroyers, both sides eventually breaking off without sustaining damage. In a second sortie, on the night of 24/25 November, the German destroyers sank two small freighters off Plymouth, and on the night of 28/29 November, the German warships sank two more small vessels and damaged the British destroyer *Javelin* in the same area. During this engagement, HMS *Javelin* was hit by two torpedoes, which blew off her bow and stern, and detonated the ammunition in her magazine, destroying her superstructure as well as killing three officers and 43 ratings. Remarkably, she remained afloat and was towed into harbour, eventually returning to service after being virtually rebuilt.

Left: *Smiling for the camera. This German naval rating is treating a depth charge with a degree of contempt. The photograph was taken shortly after the occupation of Norway, when German submarine-chasers could be based in Norwegian harbours.*

Above: *German troops disembark during the invasion of Norway. Cover for Groups One and Two, the Narvik and Bergen invasion forces, was provided by the battlecruisers* Scharnhorst *and* Gneisenau; *light cruisers provided cover further south.*

Vital escorts

The first operational sortie by the first of the new class of destroyer, *Z23*, was on 19 May 1941, when she joined the *Friedrich Eckoldt* and *Hans Lody* in escorting the battleship *Bismarck* on the first stage of her ill-fated journey from the Baltic to the North Atlantic. The new-build destroyers were generally similar to the pre-war craft, although their endurance was progressively increased; the last five of the batch, *Z30* to *Z34*, had an endurance of 10,933km (5,900nm) at 35km/h (19 knots).

In July 1941 the 6th Destroyer Flotilla under Captain Schulze-Hinrichs, comprising the *Hans Lody, Karl Galster, Hermann Schoe-*

mann, Friedrich Eckoldt, and *Richard Beitzen*, was transferred to Kirkenes in northern Norway for operations off the Kola peninsula, and soon began to register successes against Soviet coastal traffic. Later in the year the 8th Destroyer Flotilla, comprising the *Z23, Z24, Z25*, and *Z27*, was also transferred to Norway. In waters closer to home, the destroyer *Bruno Heinemann (Z8)* was sunk on 25 January 1942 by one of the 1,000 or so mines laid off the French coast between Ushant and Boulogne by the fast RN minelayers *Welshman* and *Manxman*. Three weeks later, on 12 February, six destroyers – the *Z25, Z29, Friedrich Ihn, Hermann Schoemann, Paul Jacobi* and *Richard Beitzen* – passed through the Channel unscathed, escorting the *Scharnhorst, Gneisenau* and

Above: The destroyer Leberecht Maass *pictured during her sea trials in 1937. The ships of this class had a main armament of five 5in (140mm) guns; their radius of action was 4400 miles (7080km) at 19 knots.*

Right: Sailors join in a sing-song aboard the Leberecht Maass *during an off-duty spell. The German Navy went to great pains to keep its seamen happy; all manner of deck pastimes were invented, and every possible historical event was celebrated.*

Prinz Eugen in their epic breakout from Brest. The *Z25*, *Hermann Schoemann*, and *Richard Beitzen* returned to Norway later in the month, together with the *Friedrich Ihn*.

Sorties against the Arctic convoys

At the beginning of 1942, the increasing flow of supplies by sea from the Allies to the Soviet Union was giving the German Naval Staff cause for concern, and with the majority of available U-boat resources tied up in the Atlantic, it was decided to establish a strong naval surface battle group in Norway for operations against the Arctic sea routes to the USSR. On 20 March 1942, as part of this reinforcement, the heavy cruiser *Admiral Hipper* deployed to Trondheim, accompanied by the destroyers *Z24*, *Z26*, and *Z30* and the torpedo-boats *T15*, *T16*, and *T17*. The enemy now had a formidable striking force of aircraft and warships in the theatre,

Above: A Leberecht Maass-*class destroyer (right) pictured at the German occupation of Memel, Lithuania, in March 1939. The annexation of Memel was part of Hitler's vow to bring territories with German-speaking populations within the 'Greater Reich'.*

augmented by newly-deployed U-boat groups, and convoy losses inevitably began to mount. Between 27 and 31 March, PQ13 became split up due to bad weather; two of its ships were sunk by aircraft, three by U-boats, and one by the destroyer *Z26* (Commander von Berger), which was herself sunk by the cruiser *Trinidad*. The cruiser was then hit by one of her own torpedoes, which went out of control, and disabled; the *U585* closed in to attack her, but was sunk by the destroyer *Fury*. The destroyers *Z24* and *Z25*, meanwhile, closing in to rescue 96 crewmen from the sinking *Z26*, inflicted heavy damage on the British destroyer *Eclipse* before withdrawing. The remaining 13 ships of PQ13 reached Murmansk, but two were sunk by air attack on 3 April.

On 1 May 1942, during operations against the Russian convoys, the destroyer *Hermann Schoemann* was badly damaged by gunfire from the cruiser HMS *Edinburgh* and was abandoned the next day after most of her crew had been rescued. The *Edinburgh*, already hit by a U-boat torpedo, was hit by another from either the *Z24* or *Z25* with the result that she was also abandoned, and had to be sunk by other British warships.

On 16 May, two destroyers, the *Paul Jacobi* and *Z25*, sailed from Trondheim as part of the escort for the heavy cruiser *Prinz Eugen*, en route to Kiel after being damaged by a torpedo in February. They arrived on 18 May, having beaten off fierce British air attacks en route, and were consequently absent from the Arctic when, a month later, the entire available destroyer force in Norway was assembled for operations against the ill starred Convoy PQ17. The destroyers *Richard Beitzen, Friedrich Eckoldt, Karl Galster, Friedrich Ihn, Hans Lody, Theodor Riedel, Erich Steinbrinck, Z24, Z27, Z28, Z29*, and *Z30* left their bases at Narvik and Trondheim and converged on Altafjord, but the *Hans Lody, Karl Galster*, and *Theodor Riedel* were put out of action almost immediately when, on 3 July, they ran aground in company with the heavy cruiser *Lützow*. In fact the destroyers played no part in the destruction of the convoy, which was left to U-boats and aircraft.

Following the destruction of PQ17, Allied convoy traffic to Russia ceased for a time, and for several weeks the German destroyers were engaged in minelaying in Soviet waters. Then, early in November, warships of Captain Schemmel's 5th Destroyer Flotilla – the *Friedrich Eckoldt, Richard Beitzen, Z27*, and *Z30* – set out to intercept 13 Russian ships sailing independently from Reykjavik, Iceland, to Murmansk and Archangel. The tanker *Donbass* and the submarine-chaser *BO78* were located and sunk by *Z27*.

The German destroyers' next surface action against British warships took place in December 1942, during the action that became

Above: The crew of the Paul Jacobi *(Z5) drawn up for the destroyer's commissioning ceremony in Bremen, 29 June 1937. Note the senior naval officer taking the salute on the bridge, and the 'Admiral's Barge' drawn up alongside.*

Right: Leberecht Maass-*class destroyers at sea, August 1939. These vessels were born out of the limits imposed by the Treaty of Versailles, and were an attempt to produce a 'strategic' destroyer capable of oceanic operations against enemy commerce.*

known as the Battle of the Barents Sea. All the vessels of the 5th Destroyer Flotilla were involved in this action: they were the *Friedrich Eckoldt* (Commander Bachmann), *Z29* (Commander Rechel), *Richard Beitzen* (Commander von Davidson), *Theodor Riedel* (Commander Riede), *Z30* (Commander Kaiser), and *Z31* (Commander Alberts). Their main role was to act as an escort screen for the heavy cruisers *Lützow* and *Admiral Hipper*, which were also involved in the engagement.

The early career of the Admiral Hipper

The *Admiral Hipper* had been put to little operational use since her deployment to the Arctic. On 2 July 1942, she had sailed with the *Tirpitz*, four destroyers and two torpedo boats to attack Convoy PQ17, but the force put into Altafjord, and made no attempt to intercept. She did not make another sortie until 24 September, when, accompanied by her destroyer screen, she carried out a minelaying operation off the northwest coast of Novaya Zemlya. She was at sea again early in November, with a new commander, Captain H. Hartmann, searching for freighters bound independently for Russia; she failed to make contact, but her escorting destroyers sank a Russian tanker and a submarine-chaser.

The other heavy cruiser, *Lützow* (formerly *Deutschland*) had experienced chequered fortunes since she was renamed in November 1939. During the invasion of Norway, she was part of the force covering Task Group 5, bound for Oslo, being damaged by three hits from shore batteries; on 8 April she had a narrow escape when the British submarine *Trident* missed her with 10 torpedoes off Skagen.

Early on 11 April, however, as she was making a high-speed run back to Germany, she was hit by a torpedo from the submarine HMS *Spearfish*, which struck her right aft, wrecking her propellers and rudder and leaving her helpless. She summoned help and was towed to Kiel in a near-sinking condition, and it was a year before she was ready for sea again. On the night of 8/9 July 1940, while undergoing repairs at Kiel, she escaped further damage when a bomb dropped during an RAF raid hit her and failed to explode, a not uncommon occurrence at this stage of the war. By the summer of 1941, she was battleworthy once more, and on 12 June, under the command of Captain Kreisch, she attempted to break out into the North Atlantic, escorted by five destroyers, to attack merchant shipping. She was sighted by an RAF reconnaissance aircraft off Lindesnes shortly before midnight, and 14 Beaufort torpedo-bombers of Nos 22 and 42 Squadrons were dispatched to

Below: The same flotilla shown opposite, seen here from astern. The Kriegsmarine *began World War II with 21 operational destroyers. Later in the war, new ships came into service at a very slow rate, many being commissioned before completing their trials.*

search for her. She was located by Flt Sgt R.H. Loveitt of No 42 Squadron, who secured a torpedo hit amidships. The *Lützow* struggled back to Kiel with partially disabled engines and a heavy list, reaching harbour in the afternoon of 14 June. She was to remain in dock for six months, and Loveitt was awarded a well-deserved Distinguished Flying Medal.

A fierce engagement in the Barents Sea

It was the last attempt by a surface raider to interfere with the Atlantic convoys; when the German Navy's heavy warships once more joined battle in 1942, their focus of operations, dictated by the German invasion of Russia, was the Arctic, and it was for that theatre that the *Lützow* sailed in May 1942, arriving at Narvik via Trondheim on the 25th.

On 3 July 1942, she sailed for Altafjord to join other surface forces poised for an attack on Russian convoys, but ran aground in poor visibility. Returning to Germany for repairs, she came back to Norway in December, and this time reached Altafjord without incident.

On 30 December Vice-Admiral Oskar Kummetz, commanding the Northern Battle Group, took the *Admiral Hipper* (Capt H. Hartmann), the *Lützow* (Capt R. Stange), and six destroyers out of Altafjord to attack Convoy JW51B, consisting of 14 ships with an

Above: Preparing depth charges for use. Of the 75 British submarines lost in World War II, some 42 are believed to have fallen victim to surface attack by depth charge, and the majority were destroyed by Italian anti-submarine vessels in the Mediterranean.

escort of six destroyers and five small anti-submarine vessels. Kummetz's tactical options were limited. He was under orders not to risk a night engagement against escorts which might make torpedo attacks on his ships; he was only to engage a force weaker than his own by day; and furthermore the *Lützow* was afterwards to make a sortie into the Atlantic, which meant that she would need to conserve fuel and ammunition, not to mention to avoid damage.

At 0830 on 31 December, the *Admiral Hipper* and her destroyers passed 27km (20nm) astern of the convoy, while the *Lützow* and her escorts were 93km (50nm) to the south and closing. The British cruisers *Sheffield* (Capt A.W. Clarke, flying the flag of Rear-Admiral R.L. Burnett) and *Jamaica* (Capt J.L. Storey) were about 60km (30nm) to the north. The approaching enemy force was detected, and the escort commander, Lieutenant Commander R. St. V. Sherbrooke, in the flotilla leader HMS *Onslow*, ordered the destroyer *Obdurate* to investigate. She closed to within 7km (4nm) of the enemy ships, turning away when they opened fire.

Above: *The* Georg Thiele *was one of the* Leberecht Maass-*class destroyers that had to be scuttled after receiving heavy damage from British destroyers at the Second Battle of Narvik. She was one of four ships built at the Deutsche Werke, Kiel.*

Below: *The destroyer* Richard Beitzen *(nearest the camera) entering Brest Harbour early in 1942. The* Beitzen *was ceded to Britain in 1945 and was broken up in 1947. She was one of five ships of this class to survive the war.*

Leaving the destroyer *Achates* and three smaller escorts to protect the convoy with a smoke screen, Sherbrooke headed to join *Obdurate* at full speed, accompanied by the *Obedient* and *Orwell*, and transmitting an enemy sighting report to Rear-Admiral Burnett. At 0941 the *Admiral Hipper* opened fire on the *Achates* and was at once engaged by the *Onslow* and *Orwell*, Sherbrooke sending the other two destroyers to assist in protecting the convoy. At 1020, the *Admiral Hipper* found *Onslow*'s range and set her on fire, putting half her armament out of action, and holing her engine room. Sherbrooke, badly wounded, was obliged to turn over command to Lieutenant Commander D.C. Kinloch in the *Obedient*, refusing to leave the bridge until assured that his orders had been received.

At the same time, the *Admiral Hipper* disappeared into a snow squall. Some minutes later, at 1045, she encountered the little minesweeper *Bramble*, which was armed with only one 10cm (4in) gun, and quickly destroyed her with the loss of her captain, Commander H.T. Rust, and all his crew.

Below: Funnel detail on a Leberecht Maass-*class destroyer. These were the first German destroyers to have torpedo tubes in quadruple mounts. Their armament was constantly modified to cope with the increasing air threat.*

Above: Replenishing a German destroyer with fresh torpedoes at a base on the French Atlantic coast. Faulty torpedoes constantly plagued the Kriegsmarine; *had this not been the case, Allied shipping losses might have doubled.*

As soon as the *Admiral Hipper* disappeared, Lieutenant Commander Kinloch instructed all the destroyers to rejoin the convoy, which was now threatened by the *Lützow*, only 3.7km (2nm) away. Stange, however, decided to stand off while the weather cleared, thereby allowing a golden opportunity to wipe out the merchantmen to slip through his fingers. At 1100, while Kinloch manoeuvred his destroyers between the convoy and the *Lützow* group, still making smoke, the *Admiral Hipper* suddenly reappeared to the north and opened fire on the *Achates*, inflicting many casualties and killing her captain, Lieutenant Commander Johns; she sank early in the afternoon. The *Admiral Hipper* then turned her fire on the *Obedient*; the destroyer suffered only light damage, but her radio was put out of action, so that Kinloch was compelled to turn over command to the *Obdurate*'s captain.

At 1130, as Hartmann drew away to avoid the destroyers' torpedo attacks, the *Admiral Hipper* was suddenly straddled by 24 15cm (6in) shells from the *Sheffield* and *Jamaica*, closing from the north. Burnett had been able to follow the action by means of *Sheffield*'s radar, but the radar picture was confused, and it was not until he obtained a positive sighting that Burnett felt able to engage the German cruiser. Three shells hit the *Admiral Hipper*, reducing her speed to 52km/h (28 knots); faced with this new threat, Kummetz ordered Hartmann and the destroyer captains to retire to the west. As they did so, the *Sheffield*'s guns turned on the destroyer *Friedrich Eckoldt* and quickly reduced her to a blazing wreck, but the other destroyer, the *Richard Beitzen*, followed the *Admiral Hipper* into a snow squall and got away.

At about 1145, the *Lützow* also opened fire on the convoy from a range of 16,470m (18,000 yards), then she too withdrew as the British destroyers began an attack. There was a further brief engagement between Burnett's cruisers and the enemy force at 1230, in which neither side suffered damage; the Germans continued to retire to the west and contact was lost at 1400. Three days later, JW51B reached the Kola Inlet without further harm. That it did so was due in no small measure to the tactical skill, leadership and courage of Captain Sherbrooke, who survived his injuries to receive the Victoria Cross.

*Below: The heavy cruiser **Admiral Hipper** in a sorry state at the end of World War II. This photograph was taken as she lay in dry dock at Kiel after sustaining severe bomb damage in an RAF raid. On 3 May 1945 she was scuttled, laden with U-boat parts, but was later refloated for breaking up.*

The aftermath of the battle

The Battle of the Barents Sea marked the *Admiral Hipper*'s last sortie in Arctic waters. Transferred to the Fleet Training Squadron in the Baltic, she took part in the evacuation of German troops from East Prussia early in 1945, and on the night of 9/10 April she was badly damaged in an attack on Kiel by RAF bombers. She was scuttled on 3 May and broken up in 1948–9.

The *Lützow* remained in the Arctic until September 1943, seeing no further action, and then sailed for Gdynia to undergo a refit.

From 29 September 1944 she provided fire support for German ground forces fighting the advancing Russians in the Baltic States, joining the *Prinz Eugen* in shelling Russian troop concentrations in the Memel area, and covering the evacuation of German personnel. In January and February 1945, now commanded by Capt Knoke, her gunfire supported the German 4th Army, in action against the Soviet 3rd and 48th Armies near Frauenburg in East Prussia, and in March and April she covered the evacuation by sea of German troops and civilians from that area.

Afterwards she withdrew to Swinemünde, and it was there, on 16 April 1945, that 18 Lancasters of No 617 Squadron RAF attacked her with 'Tallboy' bombs. A near miss by one bomb tore a large hole in her bottom and she sank in shallow water at her

moorings after being driven aground. On 4 May, she was blown up and scuttled to prevent her capture by the Russians. In September 1947 the wreck was refloated and towed to Leningrad, where it was broken up in the following year.

Soon after the Barents Sea battle the destroyer *Z24* left the Arctic to reinforce the French-based 8th Destroyer Flotilla (Capt Erdmenger), and on 28 March 1943 she joined *Z23*, *Z32*, and *Z37*, in addition to several torpedo-boats, in escorting the Italian blockade-runner *Pietro Orseleo* on the first leg of her voyage from the Gironde to Japan. On 1 April they beat off strong attacks by RAF

Left: German destroyers set out from their base on the French coast. One of their main tasks was to escort blockade-runners, inbound with essential supplies, on the last and most dangerous stage of their voyage.

Right: Artificers at work in the engine room of a German destroyer, sometime in 1941. German destroyers often suffered from problems with their sophisticated machinery, and the problem was compounded in the war years by the lack of quality spares and materials.

Below: The 12 destroyers of the Z23 class were all launched between 1940 and 1942, and served mainly with the Kriegsmarine's 8th Destroyer Flotilla. They were popularly known as the 'Narviks' because of their service in northern waters. Z31, seen here, went to France after the war, serving as the Marceau. She was broken up in 1956.

torpedo-bombers, shooting five down, but the Italian ship was torpedoed by the US submarine *Shad* and had to be towed back to the Gironde on the following day. On 9 April heavy air attacks also forced the return of another Italian blockade-runner, the *Himalaya*, despite a strong destroyer escort.

Bay of Biscay and Channel Operations

From June 1943 destroyers were also used to escort U-boats traversing the Bay of Biscay on the surface in groups of four or five, to provide mutual fire support against Allied aircraft. From now on, this was to be the most important area of operations for the surviving German destroyers; although they were still active in the Arctic in the latter half of 1943 – the 5th and 6th Destroyer Flotillas took part in the bombardment of Spitzbergen in September, for example, and the 4th Destroyer Flotilla (Capt Johannesson) formed the destroyer screen for the battlecruiser *Scharnhorst* during her final action in December off North Cape – there would now be

Below: View looking aft at the fire control station at the bridge of the destroyer Z39. The rangefinder is in the centre, partly covered, with the radar antennae beyond. Z39 went to the USA at the end of the war as the DD939, and was eventually cannibalised for the French ex-German destroyers.

Top right: Air-sea cooperation. Consolidated B-24 Liberators (right) of the US Navy keep surveillance as the Royal Navy cruisers Glasgow and Enterprise open fire on German destroyers in the Bay of Biscay, 28 December 1943, sinking the Z27.

a gradual withdrawal to more southerly European waters as U-boats and aircraft assumed increasing responsibility for the Arctic war.

There were some hard-fought actions in the Biscay area during the closing weeks of 1943, as the 8th Destroyer Flotilla joined other forces in beating off air and surface attacks on homeward-bound blockade-runners. In one of them, the flotilla commander, Capt Erdmenger, was killed alongside Cdr Gunther Schulz when the destroyer *Z27* was sunk in a gun engagement with the British cruisers *Glasgow* and *Enterprise* on 28 December.

Early in 1944 the 6th Destroyer Flotilla (*Z25*, *Z28*, *Z35*, and *Z39*, under Capt Kothe) moved to the Gulf of Finland, where the ships shelled Russian shore positions and renewed old minefields. The destroyer *Z39* was severely damaged by air attack during these operations in June. In August, the *Z25*, *Z28*, *Z35*, and *Z36* joined the *Prinz Eugen* in shelling Soviet troops who had broken through on the Gulf of Riga; during similar operations in October, the *Z28* was damaged by a bomb. In December the 6th Flotilla lost two destroyers, the *Z35* and *Z36*, which sank after hitting mines; the flotilla commander, Capt Kothe, lost his life.

Meanwhile, the 8th Destroyer Flotilla, now under the command of Capt von Bechtolsheim, continued to be active in the Channel area, and on the night of 8/9 June 1944, following the Allied invasion of Normandy, its warships set out from Brest to make an offensive sortie into the invasion area. They were intercepted by a force of British destroyers; the former Dutch destroyer *ZH1*, now in German service, was sunk by torpedoes from HMS *Ashanti*, and *Z32* was beached and blown up after a gun duel with HMS *Haida* and HMS *Huron*. On 21 August the *Z23* was destroyed in an air attack at La Pallice, while four days later RAF bombers sank the *Z24* at Le Verdon. Another destroyer, *Z37*, was scuttled at Bordeaux on 24 August. These losses effectively spelled the end of operations by the 8th Flotilla.

From the end of 1944 German destroyer operations were focused on the Baltic, where the ships operated in support of the final evacuations from East Prussia. On 6 March 1945, the *Z28* was bombed and sunk at Sassnitz; on 8 May the destroyers *Karl Galster*, *Friedrich Ihn*, *Hans Lody*, *Theodor Riedel*, *Z25*, *Z38*, and *Z39* surrendered to the Allies. Some of the surviving destroyers served briefly in the post-war Allied navies, before being broken up or expended in various weapons tests.

Sixteen more destroyers (Z42–Z56) were laid down in World War II, but were never completed.

Bottom right: British destroyer crews were always looking to get to grips with their German counterparts. Here, HMS Onslow and the Tribal-class HMS Ashanti, in the background, mount an offensive patrol in the North Sea.

CHAPTER 7

ESCORT VESSELS

Escort forces became an increasingly vital component of the *Kriegsmarine* as the war progressed, and German coastal shipping was subject to savage attacks by warships and strike aircraft. They suffered some fearsome losses.

The seizure of harbour facilities in the Low Countries and on the French Atlantic coast in the summer of 1940 presented the *Kriegsmarine* with a problem that had not really been anticipated. Although much of the war material necessary to sustain the German naval presence in these ports could be supplied by overland routes, it was easier to transport some freight by sea, which meant that a convoy and escort system had to be put in place.

The problem was that there was a serious shortage of escort vessels. S-boats could perform the task to a limited degree, but they were still relatively few in number and were no match for the Royal Navy's destroyers and light cruisers which, at this stage, pre-

Above: The German torpedo boat Greif *(Griffin), one of the six* Möwe-*class vessels completed between 1926 and 1928. She was bombed and sunk in the Seine estuary on 24 May 1944 while on passage to Le Havre with other warships.*

Left: Type 35 minesweepers in line astern. The first batch of minesweepers for the Kriegsmarine *was launched between 1938 and 1939; some were later converted to minelayers, carrying 30 mines. Their combat radius was around 5000 miles (8045km).*

sented the principal threat to the German coastal convoys. As the *Kriegsmarine*'s destroyer force had been decimated during the Norwegian campaign, and since new-build ships would not be commissioned before the spring of 1941, the escort task devolved increasingly on the *Raubtier* and *Raubvogel* classes of torpedo boat, 12 of which had been built in the 1920s, and 12 more modern *T*-class torpedo boats launched in 1939–40.

The loss of a popular favourite

Of the 12 original boats – which, as the nucleus of the reborn German Navy between the wars, had a special place in the hearts of many Germans – the *Tiger* had become an early casualty, sunk in a collision with the destroyer *Max Schulz* (*Z3*) off the Danish island of Bornholm on 25 August 1939. The *Albatros* was beached in Oslofjord after being damaged by coastal artillery on 10 April 1940 during the invasion of Norway, an operation in which all the torpedo boats were involved, and a third boat, the *Leopard*, was sunk in a collision with the minelayer *Preussen* in the Skaggerak on 30 April 1940. The *Luchs* was torpedoed and sunk in the North Sea on 26 July by the British submarine *Swordfish*.

The losses were made good almost immediately by the deployment of the first of the new-build T-boats, which were assigned

153

Far left (top): Four of the six Möwe-class torpedo boats pictured at their moorings. The old pre-dreadnought battleships Schlesien and Schleswig-Holstein are in the background. This photograph was taken in the early 1930s.

Far left (bottom): Wolf-class torpedo boats at anchor in Lübeck harbour, 8 January 1937. The crews are paying their respects to Admiral Paul Behnke, Chief of the Naval Staff between 1920 and 1924, who was buried on that day.

Left: The torpedo boat Tiger wallowing in heavy seas. This vessel was sunk in a collision with the destroyer Max Schultz (Z3) north of the Danish island of Bornholm shortly before the outbreak of World War II.

to the 2nd TB Flotilla under Cdr Riede, the survivors of the *Raubtier* and *Raubvogel* classes being grouped in the 5th TB Flotilla (Commander Henne). Both flotillas were extremely active in the Channel area during September and October 1940, laying minefields to protect the flanks of their projected cross-Channel invasion routes, and also making hit-and-run sorties against British shipping. This was a hazardous time for British merchantmen making their own 'dash' through the Channel.

Two of the new *T*-class vessels became war casualties in 1940. In September the *T3* was bombed and sunk at Le Havre; she was later raised, repaired and brought back into service, only to be mined and sunk north of Hela, in the Baltic, on 14 March 1945 in company with *T5*. On 7 November 1940, *T6* was mined and sunk in the North Sea; and on 8 January 1941, the *Wolf* was lost after striking a mine off Dunkirk.

Operation Channel Stop

From April 1941, convoy protection assumed a fresh priority for the British when the RAF and the Admiralty launched a combined operation, called Channel Stop, which was intended to close the Straits of Dover to enemy shipping. The air task should have fallen to Coastal Command, but because it was critically short of aircraft, the job was taken on by the Blenheims of No 2 Group Bomber Command, which flew regular armed reconnaissance sorties, known as 'beats', off the coasts of northern France and the Low Countries. The bombers flew at low level in a rectangular pattern towards, along and finally away from the enemy coastline; this pattern was designed to surprise any enemy shipping encountered before the escorts could react, and was also calculated to be the best tactic to avoid interception by enemy fighter patrols.

Above: *The torpedo boat Greif. Many of the original boats served with the 5th Flotilla, which was based on the French coast at Cherbourg, and which operated frequently against British convoys in the English Channel.*

Right: *Wolf-class torpedo baots heading out on patrol. One of the principal tasks of the torpedo boats was to act as escorts for German coastal traffic, which was subject to frequent attacks by strike aircraft of RAF Coastal Command.*

Above: **Greif** *is leading this line of torpedo boats, followed by* Möwe *(Seagull). Most of these coastal craft were destroyed in French harbours by Allied bombing raids in the period immediately after D-Day, June 1944.*

Below: An engine room artificer snatches a welcome breath of fresh air on one of the German torpedo boats. The Wolf*-class boats, powered by two-shaft geared turbines, were capable of 33 knots. The sign on the hatch reads, 'no naked light'.*

The augmentation of flak defences assigned to the convoys, coupled with the inherent risks of low-level operations and the ability of the *Luftwaffe* to mount effective convoy protection patrols, resulted in high losses: around 25 per cent of the Blenheims involved failed to return. Channel Stop ended early in 1942, and Coastal Command once again became solely responsible for anti-shipping operations, to its cost; in the first four months of 1942 the Command lost 55 aircraft and could claim only six enemy vessels. Costly and unproductive though they were, these anti-shipping operations yielded much valuable experience and led to the formation, at a later date, of specialized anti-shipping strike wings armed with Beaufighters and Mosquitoes.

Participation in the 'Channel Dash'

On 12 February 1942, the 2nd TB Flotilla (Commander Erdmann), comprising the *T2, T4, T5, T11,* and *T12* from Le Havre, the 3rd TB Flotilla (Commander Wilcke) with the *T13, T15, T16,* and *T17* from Dunkirk, and the 5th TB Flotilla (Commander Schmidt) from Boulogne with the *Seeadler, Falke, Kondor, Iltis,* and *Jaguar,* provided an important component of the naval

Right: According to the wartime German caption, the crew of this torpedo boat are signalling that they have been sent out to escort a returning U-boat. Submarines often made the perilous voyage through the Bay of Biscay on the surface.

Below: A Wolf*-class torpedo boat in harbour. All six ships of this class were lost during World War II;* Wolf *herself was mined and sunk off Dunkirk on 8 January 1941. One boat,* Leopard, *was lost as the result of a collision.*

force escorting the *Scharnhorst, Gneisenau,* and *Prinz Eugen* in their dash through the English Channel. The *Jaguar* was damaged by air attack during this operation, which was preceded by several weeks of minesweeping work by the 1st, 2nd, 4th, 5th and 12th Minesweeping Flotillas, and the 2nd, 3rd and 4th Motor Minesweeping Flotillas in the Channel and the southern part of the North Sea.

Minesweepers: a versatile craft

As the war progressed, minesweepers played an increasingly important part in escort work. In the inter-war years, the *Kriegs-*

marine inherited 36 'M-Boote Type 1915' minesweepers, all World War I ships left to Germany by the Versailles Treaty. At various times, some of these ships were modified for duty as tenders and depot ships. All were re-numbered in 1940 to fall into line with the number sequence of new vessels. The 1915 class displaced 525 tons and mounted one 10.4cm (4.1in) gun, as well as three 20mm anti-aircraft guns, and carried a usual complement of 51.

They were succeeded by 69 1935/1939 Type minesweepers, launched between 1937 and 1941. These were larger vessels, and their AA armament was steadily increased until they mounted six

Above: *A* Wolf-*class torpedo boat. In addition to boats of their own design, the* Kriegsmarine *also made use of many Italian vessels, taken over when Italy concluded an armistice with the Allies in September 1943. Most served in the Aegean.*

Below: *German motor torpedo boats in a Black Sea port in June 1943. Germans, Russians and Italians all made use of fast escort vessels in this theatre, particularly in the support of convoys to and from the fortress of Sevastopol.*

20mm guns. Another class, the 1940 Type, was launched between 1941 and 1944 and comprised 127 units, built at various yards. These ships were simplified, coal-burning versions of the 1935 Type, and by the end of the war the surviving vessels carried a very heavy armament of two 10.4cm (4.1in), four 40mm , and eight 20mm AA guns. A further class, the 1943 Type, was also ordered; this was essentially an enlarged 1940 Type incorpo-

rating various refinements, but only 18 units had been built by the end of hostilities.

In the summer of 1942, there were frequent skirmishes between opposing coastal forces, with destroyers, torpedo boats and light craft carrying out offensive hit-and-run attacks on enemy coastal traffic. One notable action took place on the night of 14/15 May, when the German raider *Stier* passed through the Channel en route for the Gironde, escorted by the torpedo boats *Kondor*, *Falke*, *Iltis*, *Seeadler*, and 16 motor minesweepers. The force was heavily shelled by the Dover batteries and attacked by MTBs, the *Iltis* and *Seeadler* both being sunk with heavy loss of life. The rest escaped, despite attempts by British destroyers to

Below: German minesweepers exercising in the North Sea in 1938. At the outbreak of World War II, the majority of Germany's minesweeper force comprised vessels of World War I vintage, which she had been permitted to retain under the Versailles Treaty.

Right: The Type 35 mine-sweeper M1, seen here, was built at Hamburg in 1938. The Germans planned to reinforce their older minesweeping fleet with modern vessels, but most never got beyond the planning stage.

Far right: Minesweepers in the North Sea. The career of the ship on the left, M89, was short-lived; in July 1940 she was sunk by a mine barrage laid off southern Norway by British destroyers.

Right: R-class motor minesweepers. These so-called 'Raumboote' were used for coastal convoy protection, coastal minesweeping, minelaying and air-sea rescue. Depth charges or mines could be carried as required.

Below: The German minesweeper R20 (left), in Danzig harbour at the out-break of World War II. In the background is the pre-dread-nought battleship Schleswig-Holstein, which fired the opening shots of the war when she bombarded Westerplatte.

intercept them en route; the British naval forces lost *MTB220* in this action.

Escorting an important cargo

Towards the end of 1942, the first of a new class of German torpedo boat made its appearance. There were 15 vessels in all, designated *T22–T36*, and they became known as the 'Elbing' class because they were built in the Schichau yard there. Displacing 1,294 tons they were powered by two-shaft geared turbines that gave them a top speed of 61km/h (33 knots), and they had an endurance of 9,265km (5,000nm) at 35km/h (19 knots). They were armed with four 10.4cm (4.1in), four 37mm, and nine 20mm AA guns and six 53cm (21in) torpedo tubes; their complement was 198.

The *Elbing*s featured prominently on escort operations during 1943, and were involved in a particularly famous sortie in October 1943, when five boats of the 4th TB Flotilla (*T22, T23, T25, T26,* and *T27*) under Commander Kohlauf were assigned to escort the German blockade-runner *Münsterland*, making a fast passage through the English Channel with a cargo of latex and strategic metals which she had loaded in Japan. The British did

Below: The motor minesweeper, R29, *seen here at speed, was one of a batch built by Abeking and Rasmussen, Lemwerder, in 1938. All boats of this class were extensively employed during the German invasion of Norway in April 1940.*

not underestimate the importance of this vessel to the German war effort; when mixed with synthetic materials, the thousands of tons of latex she carried would enable no fewer than 22 armoured divisions to be maintained for two years, while the strategic metals were intended for aero-engine production.

British warships set out to intercept her, and the light cruiser HMS *Charybdis* made radar contact with the enemy force off Ushant at 0130 on 21 October. Her accompanying destroyers also made contact at about the same time, but no information as to the probable size and composition of the enemy force was exchanged.

By this time the Germans were aware of the British warships approaching to intercept them, and the outer screen of torpedo boats obtained a visual sighting of the *Charybdis*, which was seen turning to port. The leading *Elbing*, *T23*, immediately launched a full salvo of six torpedoes at her. At 0145 the cruiser opened fire with starshell, and her lookouts at once sighted two torpedo tracks heading towards her port side. One, or possibly both, tor-

pedoes struck home and *Charybdis* came to a halt, listing heavily to port.

By now the other German torpedo boats had joined in the action, firing several more torpedoes at the British destroyers coming up behind the stricken cruiser. *Charybdis* was hit again, while a torpedo launched by *T22* struck HMS *Limbourne*. The cruiser sank very quickly, and despite determined attempts to save her, *Limbourne* was also beyond redemption. She was sunk by torpedoes from the *Talybont* and *Rocket*, which returned to Plymouth with the other surviving destroyers.

The action had cost the British two warships, the lives of 581 officers and ratings, and had achieved nothing. Thanks to the

Below: The remains of an M-class *minesweeper at the Baies des Anges, Brittany, after being battered by Allied destroyers and aircraft. The German coastal craft, which might have interfered with Allied convoys to Normandy, were ruthlessly hunted down.*

Above: German crewmen hawling aboard a British mine which has just been defused. More usually, marksmen would shoot at the 'horns' and detonate the mine while keeping out of harm's way. Mine disposal was an extremely hazardous undertaking.

Left: This mine, which has come adrift and landed on the German coast, is being carefully handled by a disposal crew. Enemy mines often yielded valuable secrets, enabling countermeasures to be devised.

Right: Minesweepers in action in the Black Sea, May 1943. A major effort against Russian supply traffic was mounted in support of Operation Neptune, an attack by the German V Army Corps on the Soviet bridgehead at Myaschako.

Far right: A view of a Type 35 minesweeper. As the war progressed, minesweepers and other coastal craft carried an increasingly heavy anti-aircraft armament. Several minesweepers were sunk or crippled by rocket-firing Typhoon fighter-bombers.

Below: The Type 35s, seen here in September 1943, were powered by two-shaft vertical expansion engines, and had a radius of action of some 5000 miles (8000km) at 10 knots. They carried a crew of 104.

action of the German torpedo boats the *Münsterland* escaped unscathed, and the next morning air reconnaissance revealed her at Cherbourg and the five *Elbing*s at St Malo. The freighter was subsequently attacked by RAF Typhoon and Whirlwind fighter-bombers through flak described by one pilot as 'a horizontal rainstorm painted red'. Two Whirlwinds out of 12 were shot down, and two more crashed on returning to base, and the Typhoons lost three aircraft out of eight, but the *Münsterland* was damaged and her progress delayed. She eventually reached Boulogne, where she was again damaged by air attack. Her story came to an end on 20 January 1944, when she ran aground in fog west of Cap Blanc Nez and was shelled to pieces by the Dover gun batteries.

A persistent menace in the Channel

Two of the *Elbing*s involved in this action, *T25* and *T26*, were sunk in the Bay of Biscay on 28 December 1943 by the British cruisers *Glasgow* and *Enterprise*. Against smaller warships, however, the *Elbing*s proved very effective escort vessels, and continued to cause the British serious problems in the Channel area until the Royal Navy adopted new tactics in April 1944. These involved the use of the cruisers *Bellona* and *Black Prince* in the role of command ships, using their radar to direct destroyers of the newly-formed 10th Flotilla on to enemy targets, and then maintaining a constant plot of the action, using their long-range guns to engage the enemy force, illuminating it constantly with starshell while the destroyers

Top left: German T-*class torpedo boats on a minelaying operation in the Atlantic. Over 500 Allied merchant ships were sunk by mines in World War II; in fact, in the early months of the war, more Allied ships were lost to mines than any other weapon.*

closed in. The tactics worked well, and on 26 April they resulted in the sinking of the *T28*, two more torpedo boats – *T24* and *T27* – being badly damaged and forced to seek shelter in Morlaix. They broke out on the night of 28/29 April and were intercepted off Brieux by the *Tribal*-class destroyers *Haida* and *Athebaskan*. The Germans fired 12 torpedoes at their pursuers and *Athebaskan* was hit, sinking at 0442; *T27* was further damaged by shells from the *Haida* and ran aground, to be finished off later by MTBs.

It was air attack, however, that sowed the real seeds of destruction among the German torpedo boat flotillas in the build-up to the Allied invasion of Normandy and its immediate aftermath. Of the originals, the *Greif* was bombed and sunk in the Seine estuary on 24 May 1944; the *Jaguar*, *Falke*, and *Möwe* were all destroyed by air attack at Le Havre on 15 June; and the last of them, the *Kondor*, was also bombed and sunk at Le Havre on 28 June.

Bottom left: A minelaying operation in progress. Early in the war, German magnetic mines, which exploded in reaction to the metal of a ship's hull passing overhead, caused serious problems for the British, but a solution was eventually found.

Of the earlier *T*-class boats, *T15* was bombed and sunk at Kiel on 13 December 1943, while *T2* and *T7* suffered the same fate at Bremen on 29 July 1944. *T18* was sunk by air attack in the Baltic on 17 September 1944, while *T10* was destroyed in an air raid at Gdynia on 18 December. All the surviving boats were concentrated in the Baltic, where they took part in evacuating troops and civilians from areas being overrun by the Russians. On 10 April 1945, the *T1* went down in an air attack on Kiel, and the *T8* and *T9* were scuttled there on 3 May. The *T13* was destroyed by air attack in the Skagerrak on 10 April 1945, while the *T16* was badly damaged in an air raid on Frederikshavn, Denmark, on 13 April.

New-builds too late for the war

Apart from the *T24*, which was sunk by air attack at Le Verdon in August 1944, the *Elbing* boats suffered their last losses of the war in the Baltic. The *T22*, *T30*, *T32*, *T34*, and *T36* all sank after hitting mines, while the *T31* was torpedoed and sunk by Russian light forces. A few boats survived the war to be apportioned among the Allied powers.

Below: In the closing weeks of the war, minesweepers joined other classes of ship in a desperate bid to rescue as many troops and civilians as possible from East Prussia, which was being overrun by Soviet forces. Many were destroyed by Soviet aircraft.

Still larger and more powerful classes of torpedo boat would have entered service had the war gone on longer. Fifteen ships of 1,493 tons, designated *T37* to *T51*, were either newly-launched or still on the stocks at the war's end; all were scuttled or destroyed. Another batch of 12 ships (*T61* to *T72*) of 1,931 tons was envisaged; 15 of these were cancelled and the rest were either bombed on their stocks or broken up.

In addition to the vessels mentioned above, 41 torpedo boats belonging to other nations were taken over by the German Navy. Of these, 26 were Italian, seized when Italy capitulated in September 1943. The rest were Norwegian or French. The four Norwegian vessels were all returned intact to their parent country at the end of the war; the 37 Italian and French ships were used in the Mediterranean Theatre, where 26 were sunk in action or by bombing raids in harbour and the rest scuttled.

Effective coastal convoy tactics

By the time the *Elbing*-class boats were at the peak of their service, German coastal convoys were well organized and extremely well defended. In addition to the merchant vessels themselves, which were all well armed, the Germans used so-called *Vorpostenboote*

(Outpost Boats), armed trawlers crammed with flak guns of all calibres, and *Sperrbrecher* (Barrier Breaker) ships which were former merchant vessels of up to 8,000 tons.

Sweeping ahead of the convoy would be purpose-built minesweepers, the *Minensuchboote* described earlier, which were also heavily armed. For close escort there were the *Raumboote* or

Top right: The **Brummer**, *seen here on the left as part of a convoy escort, was a gunnery and mine warfare training ship. Launched in 1925, she was torpedoed and sunk in the Kattegat by HM Submarine* **Sterlet**, *on 14 April 1940.*

Bottom right: A German **Vorpostenboot** *(Outpost Boat) returning to its berth. The mission of these fast vessels was to guard the flnaks of a convoy against attack, either by enemy aircraft or coastal craft such as motor torpedo boats.*

Below: Civilian hydrographers, with their station-pointer engaged on a new chart of a section of the North Sea, provided crucial data for the minelaying operations of the **Kriegsmarine** *during World War II.*

Above: *Atlantic waves crash over the bow of an F-class escort vessel. There were 10 ships in this class, launched in 1945, but their complicated machinery gave so much trouble that they were never used in their intended role.*

Below: *German civilians cheering an F-class escort as she sails out to sea. The F class were poor sea boats, a shortcoming that restricted their operational use. Several were sunk during World War II.*

R-boats, used for coastal minesweeping, minelaying and rescue of aircrews as well as convoy protection. Displacing 140 tons they carried a crew of 38, could make up to 39km/h (21 knots) and were armed with one 37mm, and six 20mm AA guns. Out on the flanks of the convoy there would be a screen of S-boats, and perhaps destroyers or torpedo boats. Any aircraft attacking the convoy would therefore have to contend with a storm of flak ranging in calibre from the heavy weapons (10.4cm (4.13in) and 8.8cm (4.46in)) on the *Sperrbrecher*, down through 40mm, 37mm, 20mm cannon, and 7.92mm machine guns on the smaller escort craft and the transports themselves.

F for failure

Ironically, the *Kriegsmarine*'s task in defending the German coastal convoys might have been made easier, had it not been for the failure of a class of warship designed between the wars, intended specifically for convoy protection. This was the F class, 10 of which were launched between 1936 and 1937. Built by Germaniawerft at Wilhelmshaven, these so-called 'fleet escorts' displaced

Above: The F8 survived the war, and was subsequently handed over to Britain as war booty. She was broken up in the Netherlands in 1950 together with F10, which had gone to the USA. Other surviving ships went to France and the USSR.

712 tons, carried a crew of 121 and had a radius of 1158km (720 miles) at 37km/h (20 knots). They were armed with two 10.4cm (4.1in), four 37mm, and four 20mm guns and served as experimental ships to gain experience with high-pressure steam boilers, and to test hull structures designed for future destroyers. However, they were very poor sea boats, and their machinery gave so much trouble that they never became operational in their intended role. Some were converted to serve as tenders. Of the 10 boats built, *F3* was bombed and sunk in Kiel Bay on 3 May 1945; *F5* was mined and sunk in the Baltic on 29 January 1945; *F6* was bombed and sunk at Wilhelmshaven on 30 March 1945; *F9* was torpedoed and sunk off Heligoland by the RN submarine *Ursula* on 14 December 1939; and the rest were distributed among the Allied powers and broken up after the war.

INDEX

Page numbers in *italic* refer to captions

Abdiel 95

Achates 146

Achilles 63, 67

Admiral Graf Spee 59, 65
   Battle of the River Plate 63–7
   launching of *7*
   sinking of *66*
   in the South Atlantic 59
   at Spithead *25*, *60*
   training voyage *61*

Admiral Hipper 23, *76*, *124*
   Battle of the Barents Sea 143, 144–7
   bomb damage *147*
   career of 76–7, 143
   fitting out *131*
   in Norway 116, 140
   Operation Nordmark 123–5
   sinking of *Glorious* 125
   transferred to the Baltic 121

Admiral Scheer 7, 74
   Adolf Hitler visits *18*
   career of 76–7
   launch 20, *97*
   in Norway 116
   refit 67
   at Swinemünde *60*
   transferred to the Baltic 121

Ajax 63, 67

Albatross 16, 153

Alberts, Commander 143

Allied Expeditionary Force 34

Altmark 59, *63*, 68, 72

Anton Schmitt 134

Argyllshire 84

Ark Royal 31, 41–2, 65, 74, 107

Ashanti 150, *150*

Athebaskan 169

Athenia 30

Atlantic Convoy Conference 48

Atlantis 67–9

Australia
   Sydney 72, *73*

Bachmann, Commander 143

Baden 10

Balkan Air Force *54*

Baltic Training Area 38

Barents Sea, Battle of the 143, 144–7

Barham 42

Bätge, Lieutenant Commander *84*

Bauer, Lieutenant Commander 69

Bayern 10, *11*

Beatty, Admiral *7*, 9

Bechtolsheim, Captain von 150

Behnke, Admiral Paul 14, 16, *155*

Belfast 119–20

Bell, Captain F.S. 65

Bellona 167–9

Belmont 45

Berger, Commander von 141

Bey, Admiral 118–20, 137

Biber (Beaver) *52*

Birmingham 82

Birnbacher, Lieutenant Commander 87

Bismarck 23, *106*, 139
   Adolf Hitler visits *102*
   career 98–108

Bismarck-Schönhausen, Prince Otto
   Eduard Leopold von 98

Biter 48

Black Prince 167–9

Blohm und Voss *44*, 98

Blücher 23, 123, *123*, *124*

BO78 141

Bonte, Commander 134

Bramble 146

Braunschweig 15

Brautigam, Kapitänleutnant *29*

Bremse 101

Brigade Erhardt 14

Brinkmann, Captian Helmuth 100,
   101, 108–9

Bristol Beaufighter Mk X *90*

British ships *see* names of ships

Browning machine guns 87

Brummer 170

Bruno Heinemann 139

Buck, Captain Paul 77

Burnett, Admiral 119

Bütow, Captain *86*

Campbell, Flying Officer Kenneth 100

Capital Ships 69–121

Carl Peters 86

Channel Dash 111–16, 157–8

Charybdis 164

Chatelain 38

Christiansen, Lieutenant 84

Churchill Winston 108

Ciliax, Vice-Admiral Otto *110*, *111*,
   115

Clarke, Captain A.W. 144

Clement 59

Commerce Raiders 59–77

Commissaire Ramel 69

Convoy PQ17, attack on 141

Cornwall 72

Coronel 77

Cossack 68

Courageous 31, *31*

Cumberland 63, 67

D-day landings 81–2, 92–4, 150

"Dambusters" Squadron *93*

Dau, Captain *63*

Davidson, Commander von 143

Delphin (Dolphin) 55

Denmark Strait passage 100

Densch, Vice-Admiral 128, 133

depot ships 86

Derfflinger 13

Deschimag shipyard, Bremen *30*, *31*

Detmers, Commodore 72

Deutsche Werke, Kiel 20

Deutschland 7, 67
   launch 20
   in the North Atlantic 59–61
   at Swinemünde *59*, *60*
   training voyage *61*
   see also *Lützow*

Devonshire 69

Diether von Roeder 134, *134*

Diether von Roeder class 24, *131*–2, *134*
   see also names of individual ships

Donbass 141

Dönitz, Captain Karl 26, 45, 46, 50,
   55, 118

Doric Star 59

Dorsetshire 69, 108

Duke of York 119–20

Dunkirk, evacuation of 82–4

E-boats 79–95

Eclipse 141

Edinburgh 106, 141

Egypt
   Zamzam 69

Elbing-class 163–70

Elsass 15

Emden 15–16, *16*, 21

Endress, Oberleutnant zur Zee *35*

Enigma codes 40–41

Enterprise 150, 167

Erdmann, Commander 157

Erdmenger, Captain 148, 150

Erich Steinbrink 137, 141

Ersatz Braunschweig 20

*Ersatz Lothringe*n 20, *20*

Ersatz Preussen 20

Eskdale 89

Exeter 63, 65

Eyssen, Captain *70*, 70–71

F-class *172*, *173*, *173*

Fairey swordfish torpedo bombers *108*

Falke (Falcon) 16
   Channel Dash 157–8
   sinking of 169

Fegen, Captain E.S.F. 76

Fein, Captain 73

Feldt, Lieutenant Commander Klaus
   84, *86*, 88

Fimmen, Lieutenant 84

Fleet Air Arm aircrew *113*

Fleet Training Squadron 98, *131*, 147

Focke-Wulf FW200 37

Förster, Admiral *74*

France
   collapse of 37
   Commissaire Ramel 69
   enemy of the future 21
   Sirocco 82, 84

Fraser, Admiral Sir Bruce 119–20

Friedrich Eckoldt
   attack on Convoy PQ17 141
   Battle of the Barents Sea 143
   destroyed 147
   escorts *Bismarck* 139
   intercepts Russian ships 141

Friedrich Ihn 139
   attack on Convoy PQ17 141
   return to Norway 140
   surrender 150

Frobisher 92

Fury 141

G7 torpedo *84*

Galatea 42

Geneva Disarmament Conference 20

Georg Thiele 123, *145*

Gerlach, Commander 77

German Defence Ministry *18*

German ships *see* names of individual
   ships

German Socialist Party (SPD) 17

Glasgow 150, 167

Glorious 125

Glowworm 125

Gneisenau 25, 110, *111*
   career 72–6
   Channel Dash 88, *88*, *108*, 111–13,
      139–40, 158
   damaged by bombs 100
   dry dock at Brest *102*
   engine room *73*
   guns *74*
   laid down 23
   Operation Nordmark 125
   sinking of Glorious 125

Gotland 101

Graf Zeppelin 24

Greif (Griffin) 16, *153*, *156*, *157*, 169

Grille (Cricket) *133*

Gümprich, Captain *71*, 77

Haida 150, 169

Hannover 15

Hans Lody 137, 139
   attack on Convoy PQ17 141
   surrender 150

Hans Ludemann 134, *134*

Hardy 134

Hartmann, Captain H. 143, 144, 147

Harwood, Commodore Henry *63*, 63–7

Hasty 94

Henne, Commander 155

Hermann Schoemann 131, 139, 140

Hessen 14, 15

Himalaya 150

Hindenburg 11

Hintze, Captain F. 118, 120

Hipper, Admiral Franz von 18

Hitler, Adolf *18*
  plans new battleships 23–4
  Schiffsbauersatzplan 21
  starts U-boat construction pro
    gramme 26
  visits the *Bismarck 102*

Hoffman, Captain 73, *110*

Holland, Vice-Admiral L.E 101, 104–5

Hood 101, 104–5, *105*, *107*

human torpedoes (Negers) *43*

Hunter 134

Huron 150

Iltis (Polecat) 17, 74
  Channel Dash 157–8
  sinking of 160–3

Imperial German Navy Battle Squadron
  9

Italy
  Himalaya 150
  Leopardi 95
  Pietro Orseleo 148–9
  submarines 38

Jaguar 17, 74
  Channel Dash 157–8
  sinking of 169

Jamaica 144, 146

Japan
  invades Manchuria 21

Javelin 137

Jervis Bay 76

Johanssen, Lieutenant Commander 92,
  150

Johns, Lieutenant Commander 146

Jutland, Battle of 7, *7*, 10–11, *13*

K21 116

Kahler, Captain 72

Kaiser, Commander 143

Kaiserin 10

Kandahar 42

Karl Galster 137, 139, 150
  attack on Convoy PQ17 141

Karlsrühe 21, 125, *125*

Kelly 82

Kemnade, Lieutenant Commander 87,
  94

King George V 74, 108

Kinloch, Commander D.C. 146

Klug, Lieutenant Commander 88, 89

Kohlauf, Commander 163

Köln 21, *128*, 131, *132*

Komet 69, 70–71

Kondor 16
  attack by MTB's 160–63
  Channel Dash 157–8
  sinking of 169

Königsberg 21, 126, *128*

Kormoran 69, *69*, 72

Kothe, Captain 150

Krancke, Captain 76

Krüder, Captain 72

Kummetz, Vice-Admiral Oskar 144,
  147

Langsdorff, Captain Hans *63*, 63–7, *65*

Leach, Captain J.C. 105–6

League of Nations 21

Leberecht Maas *132*, 133, *140*

Leberecht Maas class 24, *27*, *123*,
  131–2,*141*, *142*, 143, 146 *see also*
  names of individual ships

Leigh Lights *54*

Leipzig 21, *22*, 131, *131*

Lemp, Lieutenant 30

Leopard 17, 95
  sinking of 153, *158*

Lewis guns 87

Limbourne 164

Lindemann, Captain Ernst 99, *100*

Linsen (Lens) 94

Loveitt, Flt Sgt R.H. 144

Löwenfeld, Dorothea von 98

Luchs (Lynx) 17, 153

Lürssen shipyard, Vegesack *81*, 82

Lutjens, Admiral Günther 73, 107, 108

Lützow 121
  in the Baltic 121
  Battle of the Barents Sea 143, 144–7
  damaged 143–4
  launch of 23
  in Norway 116
  runs aground 141
  sinking of 147–8
  sold to Soviet Union *124*

Lyme Bay 89

M-Boote Type 1915 minesweeper 158

M-class minesweepers *160*, 164

Mackensen-class battle cruisers 23

Malta 41–2, *42*, 94

Manchuria, invasion of 21

Manxman 139

Marine Freikorps (Naval Free Corps)
  14

Max Schultz 133

Meendsen-Bohlken, Admiral Wilhelm
  121

Meisel, Captain 76

Michel 77

Mirbach, Commodore von 91

Moldavia 89

Motor Gunboat Flotilla (MGB) 87

Motor Torpedo Boats (MTB's) 87, 91,
  95, 163

Möwe (Seagull) 16, *157*, 169

Möwe class *153*, 155 *see also* names of
  individual ships

Müller, Lieutenant Commander Karl
  91

Münsterland 167

Narvik, Second Battle of *123*, 134, *134*,
  137

National Socialist German Labour Party
  (NSDAP) 20

Naval Officers School, Mürwick *17*

Naval Training School, Kiel *27*

Negers (human torpedoes) *43*

Nelson 74

Neptune 42, 65

New Zealand
  Achilles 63, 67
  Ajax 63, 67

Newcastle 94

1935/1939 Type minesweepers 159–60

1940 Type minesweepers 160

1943 Type minesweepers 160

Norfolk 102, 104, 108, 119

Normandy landings 81–2, 92–4, 150

North Cape, Battle of 118–21

Norwegian Campaign 34, 82
  invasion 123–6, *139*

Nürnberg 21, 126, 128–31

Obdurate 146

Obedient 146

Obermaier, Lieutenant 84, 88

Oerlikon 87

Onslow 144, *150*

Operation Channel Stop 155–7

Operation Neptune *166*

Operation Nordmark 125

Operation Paukenschlag (Drumbeat) 45

Operation Rösselsprung (Knight's
  Move) 116

Orion 69, 70–71

Orwell 146

Panzerkreuzer/Panzerschiffe 17–18

Paul Jacobi 139, 141, *142*

Pietro Orseleo 148–9

Pinguin 69, 72

Polish Campaign *22*, 97–8, *99*

Portsmouth Navy yard *33*

Preussen 20, 153

Prien, Lieutenant Commander Gunther
  33, *34*, *35*, *36*

Prince of Wales 101, 104–6, *107*

Prinz Eugen 104
  in the Atlantic 100–7
  in the Baltic *113*, 121
  in the Bay of Biscay 150
  at Brest 108–9
  Channel Dash 88, *88*, 111, 140, 158
  launch of 23
  surrender of 131
  torpedo damage 141

R-class minesweepers *162*, 163

Raeder, Rear-Admiral Erich 14, *16*,
  18–20, 100

Ramillies 73, 106

Raubtier class 153–5

Raubvogel class 153–5

Rauenfels 134

Raumboote *162*, 170–73

Rawalpindi 70

Rechel, Commander 143

Renown 65, 74

Reuter, Vice-Admiral Ludwig von 9, 10

Revenge 106

Richard Beitzen 139, *145*
  attack on Convoy PQ17 141
  Battle of the Barents Sea 143, 147
  intercepts Russian ships 141
  return to Norway 140

Richards, Commander R.J. *121*

Riede, Commander 143, 155

Rieve, Captain 125

River Plate, Battle of the 61–7

Rocket 164

Rodney 73, 74, 106, 108

Rogge, Captain 69

Royal Corps of Naval Constructors *11*

Royal Oak 33, 35

Rucktescheu, Commander von 71–2,
  77

Russia
  BO78 141
  Convoy PQ17 *44*
  Donbass 141
  K21 116

Rust, Commander H.T. 146

S-boats 79–95, *80*, *81*, *87*, *90*, 153

Salmon 128

Scapa Flow 7, 9, 10, *11*, 14, *15*, 101

Scharnhorst 100
  in the Atlantic 72–6
  in battle with *Rawalpindi 70*
  in Bay of Biscay 110
  at Brest *102*
  Channel Dash 88, *88*, *108*, 111–13,
    139–40, 158
  final action 150
  guns *77*
  laid down 23, *23*
  lured to its doom 118–20
  Operation Nordmark 123–5

sinking of *Glorious* 125
survivors *118, 119*
at Wilhelmshaven *71*
Schemmel, Captain 141
Schiff A/Ersatz Preussen 20
Schiffsbauersatzplan 20–23
Schlesien 15, *98, 155*
at Kiel *22*
Polish Campaign 97–8

Schleswig-Holstein 15, *22,* 97, *155, 162*
at Palermo, Sicily *14*
Polish Campaign 97–8, *99*
Schmidt, Commander 157–8
Schnellboote 79–95
Schniewind, Captain Otto *74,* 116, 121
Schnorchel equipment 50, *51,* 53–5
Schuhart, Lieutenant Commander 31
Schulze-Hinrichs, Captain 139
Schütze, Commander *34*
Second Reich 14
Seeadler (Sea Eagle) 16
Channel Dash 157–8
sinking of 160–63
Seehund (Seal) *30*
Sevastopol, attack on 95
Seydlitz 23
Shad 150
Sheffield 74, 107, 119, 144, 146–7
Sherbrooke, Lieutenant Commander R.
St. V. 144–5, 147
Shropshire 63
Shulz, Commander Gunther 150
Sirocco 82, *84*
617 Squadron *93*
Slapton Sands 81–2
Spearfish 143
Sperrbrecher (Barrier Breaker) ships
170, 173
Stanlake 91
Starling 46
Stella Dorado 84
Sterlet 170
Stier 77, 160–63
Storey, Captain J.L. 144
Strange, Captain R. 144

submarines
Biber (Beaver) *52*
Delphin (Dolphin) midget *55*
Salmon 128
Seehund (Seal) *30*
Shad 150
Spearfish 143
Sterlet 170
Tarpon 77
Trident 143
Ursula 173
see also U-boats
Suffolk 102, 104
Sussex 63
Sweden
Gotland 101
Swordfish 153
Sydney 72, *73*

T1-18 155, 157–8, 169
T22-36 (*Ebling* class) 163–70
T37-51 170
T61-72 170
T3D Dackel (Dachshund) torpedo 92
T5 Zaunkonig (Wren) torpedo 50
Tairoa 59
"Tallboy" bombs *48,* 92, *92, 115,* 147
Talybont 164
Tank landing ships (LST's) 81, 92
Tarpon 77
Theodor Riedel
attack on Convoy PQ17 141
Battle of the Barents Sea 143
surrender 150
Thienemann, Captain 77
Thor 6, 72
Tiger 17, 153, *155*
Tirpitz 100, *113*
attack on Convoy PQ17 143
Channel Dash 113–16
damaged by bombs *115*
deployment 110–11
laid down 23
Operation Rösselsprung (Knight's
move) 116–18
propeller shaft *117*

Topp, Captain 110
torpedoes *38, 39,* 89
faulty *146*
G7 84
T3D Dackel (Dachshund) 92
T5 Zaunkonig (Wren) 50
Tovey, Admiral Sir John 101, 102, 104,
104, 107
Trident 143
Trinidad 141
Triton code 45–8
Trothan, Vice-Admiral Adolf von *9, 10,*
14
Trummer, Commodore 95
Tsingtau 86
Type IA 26, *34*
Type II *27,* 29
Type IIA 26
Type IX 29, *36,* 45, 50
Type IXD2 *33*
Type VII 26, 29, *39*
Type VII-C 45, *56*
Type XVIIB Walter boat *47, 51*
Type XXI *30, 31,* 55
Type XXIII 55
Type 35 minesweepers *153, 160, 166*

U1 29
U12 33
U16 33
U25 34
U27 31
U29 31
U30 30
U39 31
U40 31
U42 33
U45 33
U47 33, *34, 35*
U81 42
U110 40
U123 37
U126 69
U320 55
U331 42
U505 38, *39*

U557 42
U585 141
U878 33
U1407 51
U3008 50
U-boats 29–57, *39,* 69
construction programme begins 26
escorted by destroyers 150
in Norway 141
Ursula 173
US
Chatelain 38
Shad (submarine) 150
Stephen Hopkins 77
Tarpon 77

Versailles Peace Treaty 10, 13–14, 17,
21, *22*
Victorious 115
Voltaire 72
Vorpostenboote (Outpost Boats) 170,
170

Wakeful 84
Walker, Captain F.J. *46*
Warburton-Lee, Captain B.A. 134
Warspite 134
Welshman 139
Westerwald 59
Weyher, Commander 70–71
Widder (Ram) 69, 71
Wilcke, Commander 157
Wilhelm Heidkamp 134
Wolf 17, 155
Wolf class *155, 156, 157, 158, 159*
see also names of individual ships
wolfpacks 37–8, 46, 50
Wolverine 35

Z-class 139–43, *148,* 148–50, 153
Zamzam 69
Zenker, Vice-Admiral Hans *15,* 16, 18
Zimmermann, Lieutenant 84
Zymalowski, Commodore 93–4

PICTURE CREDITS

AKG London: 142 (t), 165 (t).

POPPERFOTO: 39, 41 (both), 49, 63 (b), 64 (t), 83 (t), 93 (b), 170.

Suddeutscher Verlag: 7, 8, 9 (both), 11, 12 (both), 13, 14, 15 (both), 16 (b), 17, 19 (t), 21, 22 (t), 24, 25 (b), 26, 27 (b), 28, 31 (t), 34-35 (b), 36, 42 (both), 44 (t), 45, 59, 60 (both), 61, 62 (both), 63 (t), 64 (b), 68 (b), 69, 70 (b), 71 (both), 74, 80 (both), 82, 83 (b), 84 (t), 85, 86 (both), 89 (both), 91, 95, 100 (tr), 101 (t), 103 (t) 104 (both), 105, 106, 111 (both), 121 (b), 124 (t), 135 (t), 136 (t), 140 (both), 143, 146 (t), 154 (b), 157 (b), 166 (b), 167, 171 (b).

TRH Pictures: 6, 10 (all), 16 (t), 18, 19 (b), 20, 22 (b), 23, 25 (t), 27 (t), 29 (both), 30 (both), 31 (b), 32 (both), 33 (both), 34 (t & bl), 35 (t), 36 (b), 37 (both), 38 (both), 40 (both), 43, 44 (b), 46 (both), 47 (both), 48, 50 (both), 51, 52, 53 (both), 54 (both), 55, 56 (both), 57, 58, 65, 66 (both), 67, 68 (t), 70 (t), 72, 73, 75 (both), 76, 77, 78, 79, 81, 84 (b), 87, 88, 90 (both), 92, 93 (t), 94, 96, 97, 98, 99 (both), 100 (l), 101 (b), 102, 103 (b), 107, 108, 109, 110, 112 (both), 113, 114, 115, 116, 117, 118, 119, 120, 121 (t), 122, 123, 124 (b), 125, 126 (both), 127, 128 (both), 129, 130 (both), 131, 132 (both), 133 (both), 134, 135 (b), 136 (b), 137, 138, 139, 141, 142 (b), 144, 145 (both), 146 (b), 147, 148 (both), 149, 150, 151 (both), 154 (t), 155, 156 (both), 157 (t), 158 (both), 159 (both), 160 (both), 161, 162 (both), 163, 164, 165 (b), 166 (t), 168 (both), 169, 171 (t), 172 (both), 173.